C. RANDALL HENNING
EDUARD HOCHREITER
GARY CLYDE HUFBAUER
editors

Reviving
the European Union

Institute for International Economics
Washington, DC
April 1994

C. Randall Henning, Research Associate, is author of *International Monetary Policymaking in the United States, Germany, and Japan* (forthcoming 1994) and *Macroeconomic Diplomacy in the 1980s: Domestic Politics and International Conflict among the United States, Japan, and Europe* (1987) and coauthor of *Dollar Politics: Exchange Rate Policymaking in the United States* (1989) and *Can Nations Agree? Issues in International Economic Cooperation* (1989). He has written several articles on the politics of economic policymaking and international economic relations and has taught international political economy at American University.

Eduard Hochreiter is Senior Adviser and Head of the Foreign Research Division of the Austrian National Bank in Vienna. He has also served at the Secretariat of the European Free Trade Association. He has lectured on international economics at the Institute of European Studies, the Diplomatic Academy, and the University of Economics in Venice and has also authored numerous articles on Austria's monetary and exchange rate policies, international economics, and countries in transition to market economics.

Gary Clyde Hufbauer is the Reginald Jones Senior Fellow. He was formerly Marcus Wallenberg Professor of International Finance Diplomacy at Georgetown University (1985–92), Deputy Director of the International Law Institute at Georgetown University (1979–81); Deputy Assistant Secretary for International Trade and Investment Policy of the US Treasury (1977–79); and Director of the International Tax Staff at the Treasury (1974–76). He has written extensively on international trade, investment, and tax issues, including *NAFTA: An Assessment* (rev. 1993), *US Taxation of International Income* (1992), *North American Free Trade* (1992), *Economic Sanctions Reconsidered* (second edition 1990) *Trade Policy for Troubled Industries* (1986), and *Subsidies in International Trade* (1984).

INSTITUTE FOR INTERNATIONAL ECONOMICS
11 Dupont Circle, NW
Washington, DC 20036-1207
(202) 328-9000   FAX: (202) 328-5432

C. Fred Bergsten, *Director*
Christine F. Lowry, *Director of Publications*

Cover design by Naylor Design, Inc.
Typesetting by Sandra F. Watts
Printing by Automated Graphic Systems

Printed in the United States of America
97 96 95 94   8 7 6 5 4 3 2 1

Library of Congress Cataloging-in-Publication Data

Reviving the European Union /
C. Randall Henning, Eduard Hochreiter, Gary Clyde Hufbauer, editors.
    p. cm.
    Papers presented at a conference convened by the Austrian National Bank and the Institute for International Economics and held Oct. 18–19, 1993 in Vienna.
    Includes bibliographical references.
    1. European federation—Congresses.
2. European communities—Congresses.
I. Henning, C. Randall. II. Hochreiter, Eduard. III. Hufbauer, Gary Clyde.
JN15.R44   1994
341.24'2—dc20   93-50829
                                                    CIP

ISBN 0-88132-208-3

Marketed and Distributed outside the USA and Canada by Longman Group UK Limited, London

The views expressed in this publication are those of the authors. This publication is part of the overall program of the Institute, as endorsed by its Board of Directors, but does not necessarily reflect the views of individual members of the Board or the Advisory Committee.

Contents

Preface   v

I   Introduction and Overview

1 Prospects for Recovery and Renewed Integration   3
   C. Randall Henning

II Deepening the European Union

2 Trade, Growth, and Industrial Structure   15
   Manfred Wegner
   Comment   *Sven W. Arndt*   33
             Gary Clyde Hufbauer   37
             Helen B. Junz   40

3 Monetary Arrangements   43
   Niels Thygesen
   Comment   *Peter B. Kenen*   67
             Massimo Russo   73
             Wolfgang Rieke   76

III Widening the European Union

4 EFTA Countries   **83**
Per Magnus Wijkman
Comment   *Pentti Vartia*   101
           Thomas Lachs   105
           Thorvaldur Gylfason   108

5 Austria in a New Europe   **113**
Helmut Kramer
Comment   *Thomas D. Willett*   129
           Andreas Kees   133
           Heinrich Matthes   136

6 Central and Eastern Europe   **139**
András Inotai
Comment   *Daniel Gros*   165
           Egon Matzner   170
           Richard Portes   172

Preface

Europe's central role in virtually all international economic issues assures it a prominent place in a large number of Institute projects. We have thus conducted extensive research on the European economy. More recently, we have also devoted considerable attention to events in Eastern Europe and the prospects for those countries as they join the global economy.

We have thus followed with acute interest events pertaining to the prospects for continued economic integration in Europe. The nearly simultaneous achievement of the single market and widespread debate over the Maastricht Treaty posed a fundamental question: would the process of integration continue or be set back? The implications are enormous for the current members of the European Union (EU), for prospective new members or associates (including those in Eastern Europe) and for the world economy as a whole in light of Europe's major role.

To help answer these questions, the Institute and the Austrian National Bank decided to hold a joint conference in Vienna in October 1993. Papers were commissioned to analyze both the outlook for the future deepening of the EU (in both industrial/trade and monetary terms) and for its further broadening (to both the European Free Trade Association countries, including Austria, and the Eastern Europeans). The papers were prepared and discussed by leading economists, officials, and other experts from all parts of Europe and the United States. Maria Schaumayer, Governor of the Bank, presented a superb keynote address.

This was the third annual conference co-sponsored by the Institute and the Austrian National Bank, and funded by the Bank. The first, in January 1991, was a session on Eastern European economic reform, and the second in April 1992 addressed the economic consequences of disintegration of the Soviet Union. Each of these conferences produced important publications: *The Economic Opening of Eastern Europe* and *Currency Convertibility in Eastern Europe*, and *Trade and Payments After Soviet Disintegration* and *Economic Consequences of Soviet Disintegration*, respectively. We hope that the current volume will make an even greater contribution.

The Institute for International Economics is a private nonprofit institution for the study and discussion of international economic policy. Its purpose is to analyze important issues in that area, and to develop and communicate practical new approaches for dealing with them. The Institute is completely nonpartisan.

The Institute is funded largely by philanthropic foundations. Major institutional grants are now being received from the German Marshall Fund of the United States, which created the Institute with a generous commitment of funds in 1981, and from the Ford Foundation, the William and Flora Hewlett Foundation, the William M. Keck, Jr. Foundation, the Andrew Mellon Foundation, the C. V. Starr Foundation, and the United States–Japan Foundation. A number of other foundations and private corporations also contribute to the highly diversified financial resources of the Institute. About 16 percent of the Institute's resources in our latest fiscal year were provided by contributors outside the United States, including about 7 percent from Japan. As noted, the Austrian National Bank provided substantial funding for this project.

The Board of Directors bears overall responsibility for the Institute and gives general guidance and approval to its research program—including identification of topics that are likely to become important to international economic policymakers over the medium run (generally, one to three years), and which thus should be addressed by the Institute. The Director, working closely with the staff and outside Advisory Committee, is responsible for the development of particular projects and makes the final decision to publish an individual study.

The Institute hopes that its studies and other activities will contribute to building a stronger foundation for international economic policy around the world. We invite readers of these publications to let us know how they think we can best accomplish this objective.

C. FRED BERGSTEN
Director
March 1994

INTRODUCTION AND OVERVIEW

Prospects for Recovery
and Renewed Integration

C. RANDALL HENNING

The beginning of 1994 marks a historic juncture for Europe, the European Community, and its successor, the new European Union. Despite a number of setbacks, economic and political integration within the European Union (EU) is continuing. This process involves, on the one hand, an expansion of Community competence to new issue areas and a strengthening of its existing institutions, or "deepening," and, on the other hand, inclusion of new member states, or "widening." Economic and political integration will profoundly change Europe and its role in world economic and political affairs. But it is now seriously endangered by macroeconomic stagnation and the clash between structural reconfiguration of the European economy and market rigidities, especially in the labor market.

Consider the recent successes of European integration. First, the Community's Single Market Program, or "EC 1992" as it was dubbed, is nearly complete. While several important directives under the single market have not been fully implemented in all 12 member states, most of the nearly 300 directives have been incorporated into national law by a majority of national legislatures, and implementation should be completed within a few years. The European Union is thus close to realizing the goal of a unified market for goods, services, capital, and labor—the so-called four freedoms.

C. Randall Henning is Research Associate at the Institute for International Economics in Washington, D.C. He wishes to acknowledge Gary Clyde Hufbauer and John Williamson for comments on this chapter.

Second, the Treaty on European Union, which was agreed by the heads of state and government at Maastricht, the Netherlands, in December 1991, was fully ratified and entered into force as law at the beginning of November 1993, after intense scrutiny throughout the Community. The Maastricht Treaty substantially expanded the scope of European cooperation in foreign policy, internal affairs, as well as in the economic field, the mainstay of integration over the past 40 years.[1]

Third, with the ratification of the treaty, the second stage of Economic and Monetary Union (EMU) came into force in January 1994—notwithstanding recent setbacks in exchange rate stabilization among the European currencies. Stage two, distinguished by the establishment of the European Monetary Institute (EMI) in Frankfurt and closer coordination of monetary policy, is intended to serve as the transition to full monetary union and a common currency.

Fourth, the geographic scope of liberalization is being substantially widened in Europe. The European Economic Area (EEA) was ratified and entered into force at the beginning of 1994. The EEA extends the Community's unified market in services, capital, and nonagricultural goods to all of the members of the European Free Trade Association (EFTA) except Switzerland and Liechtenstein. Meanwhile, Austria, Norway, Sweden, and Finland have applied for full membership in the European Union and have concluded negotiations over the terms of accession.[2] The European Union could therefore be enlarged by as many as four states to a total of 16 members in 1995, the target date for the next enlargement, or within a few years thereafter.

Even as these new landmarks are reached, however, European integration has suffered many setbacks and confronts many obstacles.

First, and fundamentally, the European economy is suffering from a prolonged recession, from which it is likely to recover only very gradually. Low growth (perhaps less than 1.5 percent) and rising unemployment (above 11 percent throughout Europe) predispose governments against taking further political risks with liberalization and economic ad-

---

1. The new official name European Union refers to the three-pillar temple established under the Maastricht Treaty. In this convenient heuristic analogy, the pillars represent cooperation in each of the three areas: Economic and Monetary Union, Common Foreign and Security Policy, and justice and home affairs. We use the term European Union in place of most earlier references to the European Community, for example, when speaking collectively of the official institutions or the geographic area of the member states. The name European Community, in this volume, is reserved for historical references to the Community before the creation of the Union and, in rare instances, for contemporary, very specific references to the single economic pillar.

2. Although Iceland is also within the EEA, it has not applied for EU membership. Switzerland has formally applied but has not pursued membership negotiations since Swiss membership in the EEA was defeated in a national referendum in late 1992.

justment and thus weaken the political momentum for integration. When recovery does occur, European governments might well experience residual difficulties in mustering the political commitment necessary to follow through on their formal obligations under the Maastricht Treaty.

Second, the treaty was ratified only through a divisive political process, which exposed strong popular resistance in many countries to further concentration of policymaking authority in Community institutions. In Britain, Denmark, Germany, and France in particular, the ratification of the treaty was highly controversial, arduous, and exasperating.

Third, the ongoing ethnic and regional violence in the former Yugoslavia has exposed the fragility of the European Union's "common approach" to foreign policy. It is doubtful that the Maastricht Treaty provisions for Common Foreign and Security Policy (CFSP) alone can overcome the fundamental cleavages among Britain, France, and Germany, as well as other member states of the Union. Although governments of the member states, France and Germany in particular, are searching for common foreign policy themes, the conflicts in the former Yugoslavia have set a highly inauspicious precedent for cohesion in the European Union.

Fourth, Economic and Monetary Union (EMU), the main thrust of the proponents of integration beyond the Single Market Program, was dealt a severe setback by the succession of foreign exchange crises during 1992–93. The departure of the British pound and Italian lira from the Exchange Rate Mechanism (ERM) of the European Monetary System (EMS) in September 1992 and the subsequent widening of the margins of fluctuation within the ERM in August 1993 from the narrow 2.25 percent limits to 15 percent (permitting exchange rate swings up to 30 percent) completely transformed the system. The retreat to flexible exchange rates in practice and the poor performance of most member states on the criteria for economic convergence laid down in the Maastricht Treaty call into question the ability of even a dedicated core group of countries to create a monetary union by the treaty's 1999 deadline.

Finally, the difficulties in concluding the Uruguay Round were blamed primarily on the French government. The slow pace of multilateral trade talks revealed a perceived trade-off between liberalization within and beyond the borders of the Union, over which many members continue to diverge sharply. The British government, for example, strongly pressed for global liberalization and enlargement over French preferences for deepening of the European Union. The difficult European reconciliation that prevailed in the last months of 1993 and early 1994 entailed an agreement to pursue liberalization within the Union simultaneously with global trade liberalization.

In sum, the present condition of the European Union and its relations to the European countries on its borders is a picture of extraordinary accomplishment coupled with serious shortcomings. There is a widening gap between the ambitions of the European Union for further integration and the economic conditions and political momentum needed to realize those ambitions. Such a gap per se is not new to European integration; the Community has always progressed by setting ambitious objectives first and securing the commitments required to satisfy them afterward, sometimes years after the target date. However, in early 1994, the gap between objectives and the demonstrated capability to achieve them appear extraordinarily wide.

Against the background of the uncertainty over the future of Europe and the European Union, the Austrian National Bank and the Institute for International Economics convened a conference in Vienna on 18–19 October 1993 to address the general theme "Europe: What Next?" The conference focused first on the prospects for deepening the European Union. The second focus of the conference was the prospects for widening the Union. In this regard, the role of Austria in Europe and its potential membership in the European Union was of particular interest to the sponsors of the conference and the participants.

Five of the papers presented to the conference appear in this volume as subsequent chapters, each accompanied by the comments of three discussants. Believing that an up-to-date analysis was needed at this historic juncture, the Institute for International Economics and Austrian National Bank have produced this book in very quick time for a conference volume.

Chapter 2, authored by Dr. Manfred Wegner, former President of the Institut für Wirtschaftsforschung Halle, focuses on the deepening of the European Union and trade, growth, and industrial structure. Wegner begins with the observation that the momentum behind Community integration has exhibited distinct cycles over the decades. The future of the European integration movement appeared as uncertain as it does today on at least four previous occasions: the mid-1950s, the mid-1960s, the mid-1970s, and the early 1980s. On each occasion, however, the movement toward integration recovered, usually buoyed by an upturn in the business cycle.

Wegner first assesses the current state of the European Union in terms of the completion of the single market, the widening of the exchange rate margins of the ERM, the European recession, and macroeconomic divergence among the member states. He observes that the effect of the present recession on unemployment has been more severe than the recessions of 1974–75 and 1981–82, and he predicts, partly for this reason, that the recovery will be anemic. Wegner next compares the pattern of job creation in the United States and Canada, Japan, and the European Community over the last 20 years, noting that European growth has been driven by productivity increases and not employment gains, in sharp contrast to the United States. The European Union, nonetheless, is lagging behind the United States and Japan in competitiveness because employee compensation has exceeded productivity improvements.

Wegner advocates a program of economic restructuring that would include the following measures: private investment promotion, wage moderation, and labor market flexibility; further external liberalization with the completion of the Uruguay Round, which can be expected to stimulate competition and cost-cutting; active labor market measures to improve the quality of the work force; and an EU-based scheme, similar to that proposed in the Commission's December 1993 white paper on employment, for financing infrastructure projects specifically designed to build transportation and communication links between Western Europe and Central and Eastern Europe. In Wegner's view, the increased competition owing to liberalization and the shedding of labor by European enterprises, however, will compound the unemployment problem and prolong the recession for the next several years.

In chapter 3, Professor Niels Thygesen of the University of Copenhagen discusses the deepening of the European Union in terms of its monetary arrangements. Thygesen, who was also a member of the committee that produced the Delors Report laying out the three-stage plan toward monetary union, stresses that completing the monetary union more or less on schedule is a realistic possibility. His chapter reviews the recent crises in the ERM, assesses the present wide bands of the system, and surveys the routes for further progress toward monetary union in the current phase, stage two.

In analyzing the causes of the crises within the ERM of 1992–93, Thygesen argues that overvaluation of the Italian lira, and possibly the British pound and the Spanish peseta, furnished the initial impetus for speculation against those currencies. As the crisis of July 1993 approached, however, the foreign exchange markets increasingly discounted past inflation and trade performance, which had served to justify a continuation of the strong franc policy of the French government. Instead, the markets anticipated greater differentiation of future national monetary policies. The background to the crisis stemmed, of course, from German unification, large fiscal deficits, and relatively high German inflation, in contrast to steady inflation reduction in countries such as France.

The ERM, Thygesen notes, was simply not designed to cope in a flexible way with a major asymmetric shock affecting one of its participants. Thygesen argues that this design choice was correct, however, and defends the decision of European governments not to revalue the Deutsche mark in 1990. The narrow bands of the ERM might have been defended with different economic policy choices within Germany; a more comprehensive response to German unification on the part of the Community partners; and a more judicious application of the Basel-Nyborg rules for administering the ERM, above all the appropriate adjustment of short-term interest rate differentials.

As much as Thygesen regrets the retreat to wide bands, he sees several redeeming features in the present arrangement. First, the central rates of the ERM have remained unchanged within the wide bands. With wide bands, Italy and Britain can rejoin the ERM with less difficulty. Second, the shift to wide bands makes it easier for countries to meet one of the four convergence criteria for entry into the third stage of monetary union: namely, that the currency in question should be within the "normal" fluctuation margins of the ERM for at least two years without a devaluation. By Thygesen's interpretation, the shift to wide bands means that 15 percent, rather than 2.25 percent, is now the "normal" margin. Third, Thygesen argues, it should be possible to go directly from wide bands to monetary union and a single currency. Although Thygesen would prefer that the ERM return to narrow bands before proceeding to monetary union—and offers two proposals for strengthening the credibility of narrow bands if they were reinstituted—this step would not be necessary for achieving monetary union among a majority of member states during the 1990s.

The next three chapters discuss the widening of the European Union to the members of EFTA, Austria in particular, and to the countries of Central and Eastern Europe. In chapter 4, Per Magnus Wijkman, Director for Economic Affairs of the Secretariat of EFTA, addresses the implications of enlargement of the European Union for the future role of EFTA in Europe. He contends that EFTA will continue to play an important role as a way station for countries aspiring to broader European integration now and ultimately to membership in the European Union.

Wijkman describes a pan-European architecture for the economic organization of the continent, characterized by a "variable geometry" to accommodate the diversity of the wider Europe. Countries aspiring to successively closer integration would gradually move through three concentric circles, each corresponding to distinct but related governing institutions. First, countries willing to commit to free trade in industrial products but not yet prepared to liberalize trade in other areas, or not yet accepted by their European counterparts, could become members of EFTA, linked to the European Union through free trade agreements. Second, once these countries became committed to free movement of services, capital, and labor as well, they could join the EEA. Finally, once committed to economic and monetary union, a country could apply to membership in the European Union itself. This architecture calls for close cooperation among the countries of Europe.

Some European countries are at present unable to join the Union, owing to domestic political opposition (such as Switzerland and Iceland), or to opposition within the Union itself (such as the countries of Central and Eastern Europe). Wijkman suggests that it is likely to take at least a decade for this opposition to wane. EFTA should be preserved, therefore, as a safety net for current EFTA members and as an attainable second-best for Central and Eastern European countries until Union membership is practicable. Although the current members of EFTA are

postponing decisions on enlargement of their organization until the prospect of their own entry into the European Union is clarified, Wijkman
predicts that a consensus on EFTA enlargement is likely to emerge in
1994.

In chapter 5, Professor Helmut Kramer, Director of the Austrian Institute of Economic Research (WIFO, by its German acronym) in Vienna,
examines the role of Austria in Europe and its prospective membership
within the European Union. Austria and most of the other members of
EFTA have formed the EEA with the European Union, and Austria has
completed its negotiations with the European Commission over the terms
of EU membership. The accession agreement will be subject to ratification by the Council of Ministers, the European Parliament, the EU member states, and by an Austrian referendum. Kramer questions whether
the Austrian public will accept the operation of market forces, which
membership in the Union and economic liberalization would generally
require. He argues, nonetheless, that remaining outside the European
Union would substantially handicap Austria's economic advancement over
the long term.

Kramer paints the backdrop for the current debate within Austria over
EU membership by discussing Austria's postwar economic development.
Austria's postwar record is extraordinarily good, particularly its growth
and employment performance in the 1960s and 1970s. This was achieved,
Kramer argues, by Austria's policy of international openness, the cooperative climate of social relations, and its approach to economic decision
making. The so-called Austrian model combined flexible, pragmatic management of aggregate demand through fiscal and monetary policies with
cooperative wage decisions negotiated among the trade unions, employers, and government. As such, the model relies on strong, centralized
private and government institutions typical of corporatist countries. However,
although its inflation and employment performance continued to compare favorably to the EC average, Austria's economic growth no longer
led that of the Community in the 1980s. This slowdown has raised Austrian concerns about the long-run health of the economy and international competitiveness; these concerns have in turn produced misgivings
about EU membership.

Kramer points out that Austria, geographically situated at the heart of
Europe, lies at a crossroads for flows of goods and people, both along
the axis between Northern and Southern Europe and along the axis
between East and West. Geography thus makes Austria a hub for transportation and high value-added services, such as finance and engineering. It means that within 200 kilometers, firms based in Austria can reach
more than 100 million consumers. But it also makes Austria vulnerable
to migration from Eastern Europe. Membership in the European Union
might help to address this vulnerability, even while creating adjustment
problems for protected sectors of the Austrian economy. Union member-

ship would also help to reduce the historical dependence of Austria on the German economy. In one important respect, the entry of Austria into the European Union would be comparatively smooth and easy. The Austrian schilling has been pegged tightly to the D-mark since 1981, making Austria an ideal candidate for inclusion in the European Monetary Union. For this reason, the entry of Austria into the European Union would strengthen the probability that the Union would take a multi-speed approach and create a monetary union at a relatively early point among the hard-currency countries.

In chapter 6, András Inotai, General Director of the Institute for World Economics in Budapest, explores the trade relationship of the European Union to the countries of Central and Eastern Europe and assesses the bilateral association agreements between them. Inotai observes that trade between the European Community and Central and Eastern Europe expanded very rapidly during the late 1980s and the early 1990s. Central and Eastern European countries exhibited a comparative advantage not only in areas such as steel, textiles, and agriculture, but also in sectors that employ highly skilled labor. A disproportionate share of this trade is concentrated in Germany. The growth of intraregional trade abruptly slowed as a result of the recession within the Community, however, and in the past few years the Community has registered growing trade surpluses with Central and Eastern Europe.

Inotai severely criticizes the association agreements negotiated between the Community and six Central and Eastern European countries. Only in the cases of Poland and Hungary are the full agreements—which relate to trade, flows of capital, movement of workers, provision of services and aid, among other things—now in force. In the cases of the Czech Republic, Slovakia, Bulgaria, and Romania, only the trade sections of these agreements are in effect. Inotai fears that protectionism within the European Union is growing and that agriculture will become a formidable stumbling block. The association agreements, moreover, fail to provide a broad, sound basis for economic development that could reduce the income gap between Western Europe and the countries to the East. As a result, the potential for economic and political instability in the Central and Eastern region will continue. Inotai asks the European Union to play the role of an anchor for reform and modernization, by upgrading the association agreements to comprehensive, medium-term packages containing financial transfers, and a commitment to full EU membership, subject to the appropriate conditions.

The European Union, to conclude, is dealing with economic problems of two sorts. The first is the cyclical problem of recession and unemployment. The European recession has been aggravated and prolonged by the convergence requirements of EMU. The second is a structural problem of competitiveness, cost reduction, and industrial restructuring. The ideal moment to address structural problems, of course, would be at the peak of the business cycle, when corporate profits are plentiful, investment capital is high, and alternative employment awaits displaced workers. Europe, however, faces the opposite, more disadvantageous situation: it is carrying the hardship of restructuring at a cyclical trough.

Industrial restructuring, furthermore, might well aggravate sluggishness in the European economy over the near term by adding to unemployment. Recessions in the United States and Japan have been lengthened by the time required to restore the balance sheets of corporations and financial institutions. By contrast, the recession in continental Europe, which did not experience the asset price inflation of the Anglo-Saxon countries and Japan, will be prolonged by the necessity of shedding costly labor, reducing real wages and fringe benefits, and restoring flexibility to the work force.

Unfortunately, the European Union and its member states have not developed effective strategies for dealing with the mutually compounding problems of recession and restructuring. Normally, trade liberalization and deregulation can powerfully assist the process of restructuring, and that remains true in present circumstances. In the absence of stimulus or adjustment measures, however, the drive for competitiveness will lead to layoffs and increased unemployment in the short term. Rising unemployment will in turn create legal and social pressures to abate the drive for productivity increases—for example, through such devices as the four-day work week.

These economic conditions are inauspicious for further economic and political integration within the European Union. Challenges to the Union therefore come at the worst possible moment for the countries of Central and Eastern Europe. They also came at an unfortunate moment for the completion of the Uruguay Round on ambitious terms. One clear lesson for the enlargement of the European Union emerges from this analysis: the referendums on enlargement and Union ratification should be deferred until the European economy experiences a steady recovery.

The long-term prospects for the European Union are better than they appeared to be in early 1994. Optimism surrounding Europe at the end of the 1980s, was greater than that justified by actual circumstances. But the pessimism surrounding European integration today, as conference participant Joly Dixon has observed, is almost certainly deeper than circumstances warrant. The true prospects for European economic and political integration lie somewhere between the extremes. Notwithstanding a prolonged cyclical trough, the European economy will recover eventually. Greater optimism for European integration will then appear more realistic, and further progress will be politically feasible.

The role of the European Union in world economic and political affairs hinges on its response to these internal challenges. Over the medium term, there is a real danger that the Union will focus on Europe to the exclusion of global cooperation, as a consequence of Europe's formidable integration agenda. We have already discussed the difficult tasks of promoting the recovery from recession, forging needed structural adjustment, and coping with continued high unemployment. The political agenda before the Union—specifically the enlargement to the four EFTA applicants and the intergovernmental conference on institutional reform scheduled to begin in 1996—will add to these economic challenges. Although the European Union was able to conclude an outward-looking Uruguay Round agreement, the internal bargaining strained relations among the member states. All these factors will tend to direct the attention of EU officials and the governments of member states toward European and away from global problems.

By successfully meeting these medium-term economic and political challenges, however, the European Union could substantially strengthen its role in global affairs over the long term. The United States and other countries have a strong interest in creating a cohesive and reliable partner in the European Union. This will require, among other changes, streamlining policymaking within the institutions of the Union, shifting further from consensus to majority decision making, and increasing the transparency of the policy process. The 1996 intergovernmental conference offers the best opportunity to advance institutional reform and political integration. In order to maintain strong US–European relations and improve the management of the global economy and world affairs generally, the opportunity offered by the 1996 intergovernmental conference should not be missed.

II

DEEPENING THE EUROPEAN UNION

2

Trade, Growth, and Industrial Structure

MANFRED WEGNER

Europe is in bad shape. Not only are European currencies floating, but the whole European edifice is shaking. And not for the first time. The history of European integration is a history of crises. During the past 40 years the European Community suffered from several massive political and economic shocks:

- in 1954, when the European Defense Community failed;
- in 1965, when French President Charles de Gaulle refused majority voting and vetoed UK accession to the EC of Six;
- in 1973, when the European countries responded to the first oil price shock in diverging ways;
- in 1981–82, when a sustained world recession curtailed economic activity and slashed jobs;
- and finally, in 1992 and 1993, when monetary turmoil jeopardized the European Monetary System (EMS) and affected the timetable of the ambitious Maastricht plan for Economic and Monetary Union (EMU).

After each of these events, Europeans fell into deep despair, lamenting Europe's insufficient competitiveness and political will and complaining about inadequate instruments and resources, but forgetting these woes when a new recovery started. In fact, the dynamics of European

Manfred Wegner is Director of the Institut für Wirtschaftsforschung in Halle, Germany.

integration reveal a strong cyclical pattern. Progress in European integration was mostly linked to economic recovery and growth periods, which were sometimes stimulated by the prior crises. At the same time, progress in European affairs improved the growth conditions in member states. Success in Europe has been like the *Echternach* procession: two steps forward and one back.

Will the current crisis in Europe only repeat former cycles of stagnation and recovery? Or does much deeper change in national policies, in private business behavior, and in adjustment capability loom behind the current recession? Is there something more serious than a growing awareness among national policymakers that they are losing the power to influence economic and monetary affairs? Are national governments and the electorates of Europe instead becoming frightened at the gradual loss of economic and monetary sovereignty due to the EMS and the Maastricht plan? Can emerging protectionist tendencies be explained solely by current economic turmoil, by unemployment rates above 10 percent, and by declining real wages? And how important is the ground Europe has lost in worldwide high-technology competition?

It is unfortunate that the Community was showing signs of discouragement and dislocation in 1993, the first year of the celebrated single market and just when the Maastricht Treaty had been signed by all member states. The gloomy mood has not been limited to economic factors; it also reflects social and political events. The disappearance of the Cold War has weakened the need for cohesion. The revolution in Eastern Europe and German unification has created deep feelings of uncertainty and instability in Europe. Rising unemployment at home and the strong pressures for structural changes have provoked defensive attitudes and protectionist reactions.

The European Union and its member states are at a crossroads. Since German unification and the opening to the East, the European commitment toward deepening integration appears to have weakened. Perhaps Europe has to choose different priorities for the next five years, focusing more on the "real economy" and less on monetary affairs, thereby paying greater attention to internal European problems and devoting less effort to the outward symbol of European unity: namely, a single currency.

The Logic of European Integration: Where Does Europe Stand?

Dissatisfaction is growing with the process of European integration. Public opinion, academic economists, and some policymakers are becoming increasingly critical of the planned move toward economic, monetary, and social union. The change in mood is surprising and stands in striking contrast to the "Europhoria" that spread in the second half of the 1980s.

The Internal Market Program and Real Growth

The famous White Paper of the EC Commission in 1985, the Single European Act in 1986, and the implementation of the Internal Market Program unexpectedly revived the process of European integration. Underlying Project 1992 was a vast and coherent supply-side shock designed to improve the competitiveness of European manufacturing and services by abolishing all remaining impediments to free trade in goods and services and free movement of capital and labor within the Community. Europeans embarked on this bold program because they recognized that barriers separating national markets threatened to hold Europe back in the race among industrialized countries.

By mid-1993, almost 95 percent of the white-paper program had been approved by the Council of Ministers, while only 50 percent of the 219 measures had been transposed into national legislation in all 12 EC countries.[1] Not yet completed at the Council level are harmonization of indirect taxes and excise duties, freedom of movement for people, and abolition of all barriers for insurance, transport, and public procurement. Substantial success in attaining the internal market has bred new ambitions. First, the Community of 12 has expanded into an even larger European Economic Area (EEA), which will accept new members in the years ahead. Second, the large internal market is to be complemented by a monetary union at the end of the decade, as provided in the Maastricht Treaty (1992). This represents an ambitious step into a new dimension: the creation of a European Central Bank and a common European currency.

Project 1992 was one of the most successful action plans of the Community. It not only channeled public energies toward creating the largest internal market in the world (Cecchini 1988; Emerson 1988), it also prompted private firms to take the vision seriously, and a virtuous circle started to develop. The Single Market Program became a driving force for businessmen and policymakers and a topic for empirical research.

The EC countries benefited from the expected impact of the Internal Market Program long before 1992. In the second half of the 1980s, the EC countries experienced strong growth, and real GDP increased by 3.2 percent per year, a marked acceleration compared with previous periods. All EC countries profited from an unusual investment boom, and spending on machinery and equipment grew by almost 7.5 percent per year. In addition, inflation rates not only came down but also converged (table 1). The unusual performance can be explained by a number of mutually reinforcing factors: a general catchup process after the worldwide recession of 1981–82, the beneficial effects of stable exchange rates

---

1. However, a substantially larger percentage of the white-paper directives have been enacted as national legislation by a majority of the countries.

Table 1 Economic performance of the 12 EU member states, 1974–94[a] (average annual percentage change except where noted)

EC average	1974–85	1986–90	1991–92	1993	1994
Real GDP	2.0	3.2	1.2	−0.4	1.3
Real fixed investment	−0.1	5.9	−0.1	−4.6	2.0
Employment	−0.0	1.2	−1.5	−1.9	−0.5
Unemployment rate as a share of the labor force	7.1	9.6	10.0	10.6	11.2
Inflation[b]	10.7	4.8	5.5	3.7	3.0
Public deficits as share of GDP	4.1	3.7	4.8	6.4	6.1

a. Including East Germany since 1991.
b. GDP deflator.
Source: EC Commission (European Economy Supplement A. No. 11/12 – Nov/Dec 1993).

within the Exchange Rate Mechanism (ERM), and the virtuous circle created by preparations for the single European market.

EMS and the Maastricht Plan: Convergence and Monetary Turmoil

As the forerunner of closer monetary cooperation, the European Monetary System was successful in reducing high and diverging inflation rates among the participating members. The emerging anchor role of the Bundesbank and the Deutsche mark enforced a strong policy of "competitive disinflation," which proved beneficial for other EC countries by tying their hands. For more than five years, the ERM maintained stable exchange rates, avoided realignments, and led to a convergence in cost and price trends. Part of the exchange rate stability can be explained by the fact that the disturbances were not too large and arose outside Germany. This welcome but unexpected period of exchange rate stability ended in July 1992 when the unsolved inflationary and budgetary problems following German unification created instability and policy divergence. German unification came as a large shock with asymmetrical impacts on the ERM countries. For the first time, France and other ERM members (such as Belgium, Denmark, and the Netherlands) experienced lower inflation rates than Germany (table 2) and began to suffer from the consequences of competitive disinflation. Instead of rapid interest rate cuts (in order to stimulate slackened demand), the Bundesbank executed a tight monetary policy that was not appropriate for the rest of Europe. Devaluations, exits from the ERM, and a widening of the permitted fluctuation bands from 4.5 percent (2.25 percent on each side of central rate) to 30 percent (15 percent on each side) all characterized the strategic retreat in 1992 and 1993.

Table 2 Inflation rates and budget deficits in core member states of the European Community, 1989–93 (percentages)

	West Germany	France	Italy	UK	EC-12
Deflator for private consumption (annual percentage increase)					
1990	2.8	2.9	5.2	5.3	4.5
1991	3.8	3.0	6.9	7.2	5.3
1992	4.0	2.4	5.4	4.7	4.4
1993	3.6	2.3	4.4	3.4	3.8
Public deficit as a share of GDP[a]					
1989	+0.1	−1.3	−9.9	+0.9	−2.7
1991	−3.2	−2.1	−10.2	−2.7	−4.6
1992	−2.6	−3.9	−9.5	−5.9	−5.0
1993	−4.2	−5.9	−10.0	−7.6	−5.4

a. General goverment lending (+) or borrowing (−) as percentage of GDP.
Source: EC Commission (1993 forecasts).

Many other factors also eroded ERM stability. The announcement of a definite timetable for creating a European currency in the Maastricht Treaty, sharp cyclical differences in national economies, complete capital liberalization in the EMS, the sustained recession throughout Europe, and quickly rising public deficits all contributed to a growing credibility gap. In International Monetary Fund jargon (Goldstein et al. 1993), after five years of "convergence play," in 1992 private markets "rediscovered" exchange risk in light of the emerging economic imbalances and political hesitations. Expectations of quasi-fixed exchange rates, which under-pinned ERM success in the late 1980s and early 1990s, did not survive the triple blows of deep recession, external shock, and diverging policies. However, the proclamation of the death of the EMS due to the tempo-rary "dirty float" of the ERM appears premature. The core countries will probably return to quasi-fixed exchange rates during the next recovery period. At the same time, floating has increased the room for policy maneuver and will probably improve recovery conditions in Europe if large competitive reactions of exchange rates can be avoided.

European Recession and Growing Divergence

The current depressed mood in Europe finds its main origin in the gen-eral recession and rising unemployment, which will exceed the record set in 1984. In 1994 the European Union will have 19 million registered

Figure 1   Recessions in the EC-12

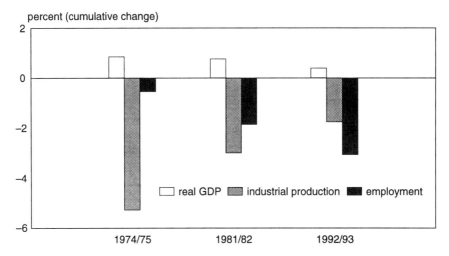

percent (cumulative change)

real GDP   industrial production   employment

1974/75   1981/82   1992/93

Source: EC Commission.

unemployed (3.3 million more than in 1992), indicating an unemployment rate of 11 percent. The slowdown of economic activity has turned out to be much deeper than anybody expected. The current recession in Europe is already as deep as the recession of 1974–75, especially with respect to the sharp downturn in employment (figure 1).

Apparently, in most member countries the decline in output is bottoming out, and in the United Kingdom signs of recovery are even appearing. But many indicators still reveal risks. Thus, an anemic recovery is the most probable outcome in 1994 and for the European Union as a whole. The reasons for the difficult recovery can be summarized as follows: moderate international demand, the large burden facing Germany in reconstructing its Eastern economy, the impact until recently of competitive disinflation due to the ERM, record budgetary deficits, and strong pressures on firms to shed labor in order to achieve lean production.

Yet even with a weak economy, inflation is edging down only reluctantly. Recent devaluations and exchange rate floating within the EMS have enhanced the danger of rising import prices and higher inflation rates in many countries. In addition, the overall budgetary position of the Community has worsened since 1989. In 1993 the deterioration was almost entirely due to rising budget deficits in the four large countries, and these will not be soon reversed (table 2). In 1993 general government net borrowing in the European Community as a whole amounted to more than 6 percent of GDP, thus exceeding the Community's previous highest recorded figure (5.2 percent in 1982). Interest payments on the public debt in 1993 represented more than 5 percent of GDP. Some EU countries are facing worrisome budgetary imbalances that cry out for radical reforms. The overall conclusion is that rising public deficits have created instabilities of their own and that the budgetary instrument is not now available for stimulating economic recovery.

Most affected by the current downturn is fixed investment, which fell in 1993. In fact, the overall investment share of the 12 EC member states was less than 20 percent of GDP in 1993. Expectations of an investment recovery in 1994 are on shaky ground. Many sectors face overcapacity and adjustment problems. Unlike other recovery episodes, the European Union cannot rely upon strong external demand from neighboring countries. Most EU countries are suffering from weak exports caused by cyclical factors among the main European trading partners as well as from a gradual erosion of Europe's competitiveness. The growth regions lie far from the EU countries. Thus, boosting exports will necessarily involve a new trade strategy.

Key Policy Areas and Priorities for Europe

At the end of 1992, the European Council called on member states—in its usual discreet and subtle rhetoric—to take action to "boost confidence and promote recovery." The Edinburgh initiative invited the EC countries to take concerted action in three main areas:

- exploiting the available margins for maneuver in fiscal policy to encourage private investment and to switch public expenditure toward infrastructure and other growth-supporting priorities;

- strengthening structural adjustment efforts—for example, through actions to reduce subsidies, to enhance competition, and to improve market flexibility;

- promoting wage moderation, with particular regard to the public sector, given the important demonstrative role it plays and the positive effects on budgetary consolidation.

All these actions may be justified under current circumstances, but most member states feel tightly constrained by budgetary problems and adjustment pressures. The current debate in most countries is focused both on the structural policies mentioned above and on how to cut large budgetary deficits (as in Italy) without damaging economic activity. Demand stimulus in Europe will not come from private or public consumption, as most countries are necessarily undergoing a long period of wage moderation and shrinking employment. Private investment growth will probably start only when firms regain their confidence and prepare for new products and expanding markets inside and outside the European Union.

Against this difficult background, an efficient medium-term strategy for the Union should be based on the fundamental interrelationship between macroeconomic policies, structural adjustment, and trade-opening policies.

Growth and Employment: Unsolved Issues

Notwithstanding some improvements, which took place during the 1980s (for example, in inflation and profitability), EU growth potential appears to remain low. Most forecasts reveal a modest medium-term growth rate around 2.0 to 2.5 percent per year for the Union as a whole (Delessy and Sterdyniak 1993). However, a slow-growth scenario will not solve the serious and persistent unemployment problem that emerged recently in almost all the member countries. The employment threshold (defined as the minimal rate of growth of real GDP that must be reached before total employment starts growing) has remained remarkably stable at around 2.0 percent for the Union as a whole (Commission of the European Communities 1993a). Given the most likely development for labor supply (rising by 0.5 percent per year) and the existing high unemployment rate (12 percent), an attractive solution would entail strong and sustainable growth with an average increase of real GDP of around 3.0 to 3.5 percent for several years.

It is often argued that sustainable annual growth rates of 3.0 to 3.5 percent are difficult to achieve and that growth alone will not be able to raise the level of employment in Europe. While the strong employment performance of the Community between 1986 and 1990 (1.2 percent growth per annum) was linked to high growth rates of real GDP (3.2 percent per annum; see Commission of the European Communities 1991b), in general, European growth has been driven by productivity increases and not by employment expansion (in contrast to the United States). In the 1960s and 1970s, European countries experienced low employment growth and low participation rates (today less than 60 percent of the EU population of working age is employed, compared with more than 70 percent in the United States, Japan, and the countries of the European Free Trade Association). The diverging employment record can be explained by different patterns in real wage rates and the creation of private-sector jobs in North America and Japan, by comparison with the emphasis on public-sector jobs in the Union (figure 2).

The rapid private-sector job creation in North America has been achieved in part through deregulated and flexible labor markets. Compared with Europe, this job growth entailed low labor productivity and stagnant real wage growth (Wegner 1983). For these reasons, it must be questioned whether Europe could easily follow the US model in order to solve its own unemployment problems.

Figure 2 US and Canada, Japan, EC: jobs created, 1973-91

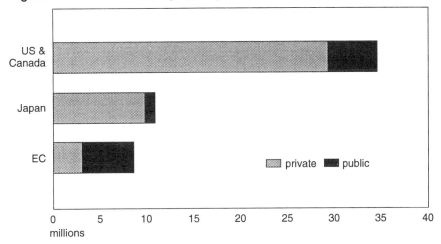

Source: OECD.

A strong growth performance can be justified by other reasons besides meeting a minimum target of EU job creation. In Germany, the burden of unification and the risks of disruptive labor inflows can only be absorbed by high growth rates. In France, a shift toward higher growth and employment seems urgent now that price and wage inflation have been arrested at the price of very high unemployment (Blanchard and Muet 1993). In general, faster GDP growth implies higher investment ratios and rising profitability owing to modest wage increases and more efficient and flexible labor supply practices. The optimal policy design consists of strengthening internal and external competition, both to promote higher efficiency and flexibility in the use of productive factors (especially labor) and to eliminate rigidities that hinder industrial change. The internal component could be handled by a stronger drive toward completing the single-market initiative, while the external component could emerge from a consistent and courageous trade-opening policy. By revitalizing the internal market and external growth approaches, the European Union can stem and even reverse the widespread Europessimism that now dampens expectations and investment plans.

A loosely coordinated policy of promoting better growth conditions and more job creation has to focus on at least four key areas:

■ reducing bureaucracy and public intervention in investment and innovation (this requires a reduction of subsidies and less public assistance for rent-seeking activities) and increasing the flexibility of labor markets;

■ moderating wage increases to support a job-creating growth strategy (similar to the efforts of the late 1980s), combined with instituting measures for sharing the rising wealth accumulation in the 1990s among employees;

- intensifying active labor market and innovation measures such as education, training, and research and development to improve the quality of the labor force;

- developing an EU-based scheme for financing large infrastructure projects to link (mainly though transport and communication) Western Europe and the reform countries in Central and Eastern Europe.

Competitiveness and Industrial Change: Lagging Behind in Europe

The deep recession in most EU countries has revealed a number of structural deficiencies. During the past five years and in contrast to the United States, Japan, and the newly industrialized countries, the Community has lost export markets. The decline in Europe's share of world exports and the persistent Community trade deficit vis-à-vis the rest of the world can be partly explained by cyclical and special factors (e.g., German unification) and partly by the loss of cost competitiveness due to rising labor costs and overvaluation against the dollar since 1987. Many European firms have neglected fast-growing markets (notably in Asia and Latin America) and new high-tech areas. Supply-oriented policies and institutional reforms (affecting, for example, corporate and personal taxes and the social security system) have been modest. Some of the countries (such as Germany) are gradually losing the advantage of important historical competitive factors, such as outstanding university education and exceptional R&D intensity. Some urgent policy tasks, such as cutting subsidies and accelerating privatization, have been implemented only with hesitation. In fact, the restructuring of most European economies has proceeded with caution and restraint.

Global competitive conditions are now characterized by increased capital mobility and rapid flows of technical knowledge based on the microelectronic revolution. Locational competition (*Standortwettbewerb*) within Europe has been intensified by the existence of extremely low-wage countries at the EU's doorstep, especially from the reform countries in Central and Eastern Europe. The rapid shift of production from high-wage to low-wage locations is possible and profitable not only for labor-intensive consumer goods, but also for middle-technology products and even for some services, such as software.

One of the worrying macroeconomic factors in most large EU countries is the rapid deterioration of the budget position since 1989 (table 2), and again, in comparison with the United States. At the same time, the share of taxes and social insurance contributions, expressed as a percent-

Figure 3 Public expenditure and tax ratios in 1992

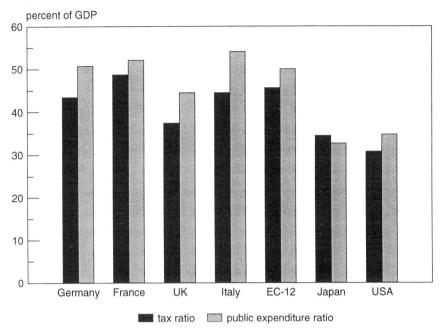

percent of GDP

■ tax ratio   ▨ public expenditure ratio

Sources: OECD, EC, and SIBA.

age of GDP, is much higher in the European core countries than in the United States and Japan (figure 3), and it has increased markedly in recent years.

Trade: Internal Market and the Uruguay Round

The strategic policy for deepening European economic integration was based on internal trade liberalization in three phases: elimination of customs duties and quantitative restrictions, successive enlargements from six to twelve members, and completion of the internal market (Sapir 1992). The result has been a spectacular growth of intra-Community trade shares, jumping from less than 40 percent in 1958 to almost 55 percent in 1970 and, after a stagnation lasting until 1985, rising to more than 60 percent in 1992.

There are strong links between overall GDP growth, market opening (including the accession of new members), and intra-European trade expansion (mainly through intra-industry specialization). However, the volume growth of extra-Community exports to the rest of the world was extremely modest during the second half of the 1980s (0.6 percent growth per year), while extra-EC imports increased markedly during this growth

Figure 4 Growth of EC trade volumes, 1979–94

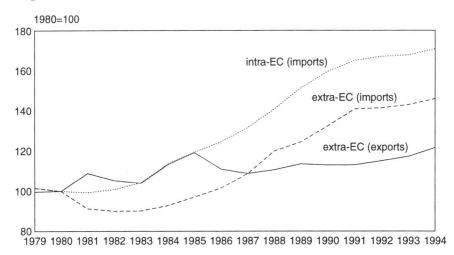

1980=100

Sources: Eurostat and author's calculations.

period (7 percent per year; figure 4). The rapid growth of extra-EC imports in the second half of the 1980s provides some evidence against the "Fortress Europe" thesis. Extra-EC import expansion has been especially strong for imports of manufactured goods (growing by 9 percent per year), reflecting the German unification boom (Commission of the European Communities 1993a).

European integration and trade expansion furnished the locomotive for overall growth in the Community and also provided the base for large improvements in living standards. It is doubtful whether intra-EC trade expansion will continue in the near future at the same pace as in the past. The reasons for this are a weak recovery and slowing integration due to private-sector uncertainties about further progress.

The way out of this impasse is to rely upon the internal-market initiative, to accelerate external trade liberalization by rapidly accepting new members (enlargement), and through the trade barrier reductions negotiated in the Uruguay Round. The impact of ratifying the new and wide-ranging GATT rules will be less immediate than expected, but it will encourage traders and investors in the medium term. The European Union as a whole stands to benefit most from improved market access. Some GATT and EU estimates indicate the creation of roughly 90,000 to 130,000 additional jobs a year over 10 years. The Union would also profit from trade liberalization where the Single Market Program in services "is likely to be a driving force for exploiting the 'sleeping' opportunities of the General Agreement on Trade in Services" (Messerlin 1993). Stronger European performance in financial and production-oriented services could compensate for losses in more traditional industries. Alternatively, if the European Union turns to the use of neoprotectionist devices, that would delay inevitable structural change and countermand Europe's GDP growth and employment expansion.

There are lessons to be learned from the monetary turmoil since September 1992. Progress toward Maastricht in the monetary field is only possible through greater economic convergence. One prerequisite is strong, growth-oriented European countries, which are able to face the twin challenge of higher employment without inflation and greater competitiveness. During the conclusion of the Uruguay Round, EU members, especially Germany, convinced France that the combination of internal and external liberalization could be a powerful means for strengthening competition and enhancing growth conditions. Because the influence of GATT rules on French foreign trade is much smaller than for most other countries (less than 25 percent of French exports are subject to GATT rules), France was persuaded. Furthermore, French agricultural exports, a stumbling block to the negotiations, benefited from substantial aids derived from the Common Agricultural Policy. The CAP, an expansive and distorting sectoral policy that absorbs 60 percent of the EU budget, should be reformed in any case.

Central and Eastern Europe: New Opportunities

The reform efforts in Central and Eastern Europe and the EC association agreements to open trade with these countries have created opportunities for both sides. "Trade not aid" should become the European slogan for economic transformation.

In 1989, EC trade with countries in Central and Eastern Europe and the former Soviet Union accounted for only 6 to 7 percent of total extra-Community trade. However, for the Central and Eastern European countries, including Bulgaria, the Czech Republic, Hungary, Poland, Slovakia, and Romania, overall trade with the West was already important in the pretransition period and in 1989 represented 15 to 30 percent of their exports. The European Union has become and will remain the largest trading partner for most of the reform countries of Central and Eastern Europe (already accounting for more than 50 percent of their total exports).

Between 1989 and 1992, the three reform countries—Poland, Hungary, and former Czechoslovakia—increased their Western exports by 40 to 56 percent (mostly to the European Community). These gains compensated for the loss of Eastern markets. In the same period, West German imports from the Central and Eastern European reform countries increased by 58 percent, whereas East German imports from these countries fell by 83 percent (Wohlers 1993). But at the end of 1992, export growth from the transition countries began to slow (with the exception of the Czech Republic) due to the recession in the main European countries. In the first half of 1993, exports from Poland, Hungary, and Bulgaria actually declined.

The main reasons for the rapid trade expansion up until 1993 have been the favorable demand conditions in most EC countries in 1990–91, the large requirements for capital equipment in Eastern countries, their highly competitive exchange rates, and the massive labor-cost differentials. Wage costs in former Czechoslovakia, Poland, and Hungary represent today only a fraction of Western costs (between 3 and 9 percent of West Germany's monthly wage level, for example; see Richter 1993).

The integration of the Central European countries in the new international division of labor has been and will continue to be promoted by preferential access to the EU market. The new trade and cooperation agreements and the more recent association agreements offer immediate market access, but the European Union is still protecting its sensitive products, especially farm products, iron and steel, textiles, clothing, footwear, and chemicals (Commission of the European Communities 1993a). These sectors represent an important part of the export supply in the Visegrád countries; for example, the industrial sectors in question accounted for 35 to 40 percent of manufacturers' value added in Czechoslovakia, Hungary, and Poland in 1989. The Union will open its "sensitive industrial markets" only gradually but has recently made some concessions. It is sometimes feared (Winters 1993) that the arrangements constitute "managed trade"—often nontransparent, bureaucratic, and open to increasing discrimination with respect to third countries. Such arrangements run counter to the key element of transformation: a changed role for government (Ostry 1993).

Trade between Eastern Europe and the European Union will not be a one-way affair but will create strong demand for Western European goods. Some studies suggest very large potential for trade growth (by factors between 2.5 and 10) between Eastern European countries and the Union after full, long-term adjustment (Hamilton and Winters 1992).[2] In the Union, the price of expanded trade is temporary adjustment costs, including job losses, in some sensitive sectors. However, it is probably true that the shock of competition from Eastern Europe is manageable and "well within the range of the normal experience of economic change" (Rollo and Smith 1993; NERA 1993). Nevertheless, a radical opening of the EU market will likely be opposed by the southern EU members because their trade structure in manufactured goods is similar to that of the Eastern countries.

---

2. A detailed study on trade and foreign investment in Central and Eastern Europe, including the former Soviet Union, has confirmed the favorable perspective. An optimistic scenario generates a very substantial increase in the trade of these countries with the European Union: between 1991 and 2010, a fivefold increase in their exports to the Union and a sevenfold increase in their imports from the Union (NERA 1993).

Unfortunately, a more rapid trade liberalization program will affect the ailing industrial sectors in eastern Germany and accelerate the ongoing deindustrialization. Therefore, the European Union (and not only western Germany) has to provide adjustment assistance in order to facilitate the abrupt structural change and to create modern industries. Assistance to eastern Germany is also warranted by the fact that its per capita GDP amounts to only 35 to 40 percent of the EU average (far below the level of the poorest EU countries, Portugal and Greece).[3]

Failure to transform eastern Germany and the reform countries in Central and Eastern Europe will have serious repercussions on European integration and could endanger peace and prosperity in Europe. The situation will become even more urgent if the countries of the former Soviet Union experience further economic chaos and political instability. Thus, support for the economic and political transition of Central and Eastern European countries has to receive a high priority in EU policies in the years ahead. Large EU-financed infrastructure programs could improve the growth conditions in this region and contribute to faster growth in the European Union.

Conclusions

A worrisome feeling is creeping about that the crisis is more than a temporary cyclical phenomenon. The current Europessimism contrasts with the undeniable progress in integrating an ever-increasing number of national economies within the EU framework. The deepening of European economic integration was achieved by several steps toward internal trade liberalization. Despite this evident progress, EU member states seem to have lost confidence in the advantages of deepening.

The current pessimism is a consequence of the cyclical pattern in liberalizing markets for goods and factors. This pessimism can be explained by three main economic factors: as a reaction to the overoptimism created by Europe 1992, by the recent shock of the crumbling Exchange Rate Mechanism, and by the general recession and depressed business climate coupled with fundamental deficiencies in adjusting to external competitive pressures. The European Union has few attractive alternatives in shaping its immediate future. Few member countries are prepared to risk bold and rapid steps toward monetary and political integration. After recent experience with the ERM, it even seems difficult to stick to the timetable of the Maastricht plan.

---

3. The recent extension of the European Structural Fund for 1994–99 will provide eastern Germany with 14 billion ECU, which in relative terms is much less than the support provided to Spain, Portugal, and Greece from the Cohesion Fund.

There is within Europe a temptation to respond to rising competitive pressures in trade and in capital markets with a retreat toward the internal market, explicitly embracing the concept of economic regionalism. So far, the Union has acted as a countervailing force against these tendencies, the ambitious and difficult construction of Europe has been successful, and the Union has generally pursued a liberal external trade policy (Sapir 1992). The task now is to maintain and reinforce an outward orientation even during difficult times. The dynamics of the single-market initiative should be reestablished by combining internal liberalization efforts with the effects of enlargement and open trade policies.

The most urgent priority in policymaking is to promote a rapid recovery in Europe through sustained economic growth. Progress in unifying Europe is only possible when efforts at reducing unemployment are successful. In the recent past, most European countries have been reluctant to implement structural changes and to reform their expensive welfare and social systems. The prolonged recession and structural deficiencies have served as an eye-opener that industrial change is inevitable. The recession offers a unique opportunity to eliminate some of the deadweight and social burden, which most countries are unable to afford.

The Union should resist the temptation to use protectionist measures as a short-term stopgap. Protection would only delay the inevitable structural change and make the final outcome more painful and expensive. The Union should also check the tendency of member states to retreat to protective measures at a national level. Europe has reached a degree of interdependence that makes spillover effects almost automatic and national solutions unrewarding. Until 1993, the Community followed a pragmatic but somewhat muddled approach to trade policy. Successful conclusion of the GATT negotiations represents a breakthrough that could improve the business climate and Europe's growth potential.

One of the new factors shaping Europe has been the unexpected emergence of reform countries in Central and Eastern Europe. They require technical and financial help and open markets for their exports. A much more open external trade policy vis-à-vis Central and Eastern European countries would encourage their efforts at economic reform, improve their political stability, and prepare the ground for very large two-way trade growth. Instead of dispersed financial help, the European Union should focus its support on communication and traffic networks to provide a modern infrastructure in Central and Eastern Europe that will link those countries to the EU member states.

Over the next few years, the European Union may need to concentrate its energy on consolidating and finalizing the Single Market Program, on streamlining internal decision-making mechanisms, and on improving transparency and accountability so as to reduce the democratic deficit. Most member-state governments have so far failed to sell their plans for European construction to the broader European public. More time and effort is required. As Jean Monnet expressed it: "The construction of Europe, like all peaceful revolutions, needs time—time to convince, time to adapt people's thinking and time to adjust to the great transformations" (quoted in Goldstein 1992).

References

Blanchard, Olivier Jean, and Pierre Alain Muet. 1993. "Competitiveness through disinflation: an assessment of the French macroeconomic strategy." *Economic Policy* 16 (April). Cambridge, UK: Cambridge University Press.

Cecchini, Paolo, et al. 1988. *The European Challenge 1992:* The Benefits of a Single Market. Aldershot (England): Wildwood House for the EC Commission.

Centre for Economic Policy Research. 1990. *Monitoring European Integration: The impact of Eastern Europe.* London: CEPR.

Commission of the European Communities. 1991a. "Annual Economic Report 1991–92." *European Economy* 50, no. 3. Brussels.

Commission of the European Communities. 1991b. "Developments on the EC labor market since 1983." *European Economy* no. 50. Brussels.

Commission of the European Communities. 1993a. "The European Community as a world trade partner." *European Economy* no. 52. Brussels.

Commission of the European Communities. 1993b. "Annual Economic Report for 1993." *European Economy* no. 54. Brussels.

Delessy, H., and H. Sterdyniak. 1993. "Croissance: le secret perdu? Une projection de l'économie mondiale 1993–2000." *Observations et diagnostics économiques* 46. Paris: Revue de l'OFCE (July).

Emerson, Michael, et al. 1988. "The Economics of 1992: An Assessment of the Potential Economic Effects of Completing the Internal Market of the European Economy." *European Economy*, no. 35. Luxembourg: European Communities Directorate-General for Economic and Financial Affairs (March).

Goldstein, Walter. 1992. "Europe after Maastricht." *Foreign Affairs* 71, no. 5.

Goldstein, Morris, David Folkerts-Landau, Peter Garber, et al. 1993. *International Capital Markets*—Part I: Exchange Rate Management and International Capital Flows. Washington: International Monetary Fund.

Hamilton, Carl, and L. Alan Winters. 1992. "Opening up international trade with Eastern Europe." *Economic Policy* 14 (April). Cambridge, UK: Cambridge University Press.

Messerlin, A. 1993. "Services." *European Economy* no. 52. Brussels.

National Economic Research Associates (NERA). 1993. "Trade and foreign investment in the Community's regions: the impact of reform in Central and Eastern Europe." *Regional Development Studies* 7. Brussels: Commission of the EC.

Ostry, Sylvia. 1993. *The Threat of Managed Trade to Transforming Economies.* Occasional Paper 41. Washington: Group of Thirty.

Rollo, Jim, and Alasdair Smith. 1993. "The political economy of Eastern European trade with the European Community: why so sensitive?" *Economic Policy* 16 (April). Cambridge, UK: Cambridge University Press.

Richter, Sándor. 1993. *East-West trade under growing western protectionism.* Vienna: Vienna Institute for Comparative Economic Studies.

Sapir, André. 1992. *Regional Integration in Europe.* Economic Papers No. 94. Brussels: Commission of the European Communities (September).

Wegner, Manfred. 1983. *The employment miracle in the US and stagnating employment in the EC*. Economic Papers No. 17. Brussels: Commission of the European Communities.

Winters, L. Alan. 1993. "The European Community: a case of successful integration?" In Jaime de Melo and A. Panagariya, *New Dimensions in Regional Integration*. Cambridge, UK: Cambridge University Press.

Wohlers, Eckhardt. 1993. "Tendenzen im Handel mit den Ländern Mittel- and Osteuropas." *Wirtschaftsdienst* VIII/93. Hamburg.

Comment

SVEN W. ARNDT

The European Union is passing through difficult times. Recession, persistently high unemployment, and troubles in the exchange rate system are among the problems Wegner analyzes. His paper and the contemporary policy debate in Western Europe are reminiscent of the early 1980s, which also witnessed Eurosclerosis and Europessimism. Then, too, the debate centered on the causes of economic sluggishness and high unemployment, and the extent to which these symptoms represented structural rather than cyclical problems. The argument was never resolved. Europeans simply lost interest as their economies revived under the stimulus of the Europe 1992 initiative. Despite this initiative and the ongoing internal market program, economic activity is languishing and high unemployment persists. This leaves Europeans no choice but to revisit the old debate.

The arguments are familiar. As before, the problem is partly macroeconomic and cyclical, and the cyclical component is intensified by worldwide recession. However, the dilemma for EU policymakers is that the accumulation of budget deficits when times were good has limited the leverage countercyclical fiscal policy ought to provide now that times are bad. Clinging to ERM-mandated parities has only exacerbated the problem. Although Wegner worries about floating EU currencies, he understands that greater flexibility in rates might be just what the doctor would order when other policy options are severely limited.

Sven W. Arndt is C. W. Stone Professor of Money, Credit and Trade and Director of the Lowe Institute of Political Economy at Claremont McKenna College.

It is also clear that Europe's current problems are more than just cyclical. Unemployment, for example, was persistently high even before the downturn. Once again, Western Europeans are asking to what extent factor-market rigidities and high and rising labor costs have made their economies internationally uncompetitive and what role if any the complex European welfare state has played in this development. Wegner notes that, despite the stimulus of Europe 1992, the principal growth areas of the world remain outside the European Union. Thus, the focus naturally shifts to EU trade policies.

Although the European Union has been an active participant in multilateral trade liberalization under the GATT, a large share of its attention has been devoted to internal trade liberalization and intra-EU policy integration. Western European economic and trade policies thus have an inward-looking bias. Although these policies have not taken on the Fortress Europe flavor that many feared, they have been and are increasingly becoming defensive and protective. Even now, in an effort to keep the bicycle of European integration from tipping over, leaders in the European Union are searching for a new intra-EU initiative to shake Europe out of the doldrums. Regrettably, very few Europeans seem to see much stimulative promise in extra-EU trade initiatives such as the recently completed Uruguay Round.

An inwardly oriented approach may very well work again. While it suffers from diminishing returns, this approach suits the modern Western European mind-set. Europeans like the idea of boosting growth by means of economic deepening within the region. And even when they look for external stimuli for this growth, they prefer EU-widening initiatives to nondiscriminatory approaches. Deepening and widening are appealing in part because they enable Western Europe to ensure much-coveted reciprocity. This helps explain the broad political support for restricting access to agricultural products, textiles, steel, and other "sensitive" products from Central and Eastern Europe until those countries have been fully admitted into the Union.

But pushing preferential liberalization and admitting neighboring countries makes less sense as the European Union expands. First of all, a larger number of members may complicate administration and decision making within the European Union. Second, given the extent of deepening already in place, new entrants must buy into more than just trade liberalization; this makes assimilation more problematic. Third, as the European Union extends its regional frontiers, it tends to capture increasingly less-industrialized and less-developed neighbors. The new members increase the demands for income transfers, which in turn increases the costs of widening for existing members. By contrast, multilateral liberalization may offer increasingly attractive cost-benefit ratios. Finally, less-industrialized EU members will tend to be more protectionist in the multilateral arena as they try to defend their industries against competition from industrializing outsiders with similar production structures. Additional widening of the European Union thus promises to increase its bias against multilateralism.

If widening is nevertheless the preferred approach, why must it involve full membership? Could new entrants join the EU customs union but not its common market, for example? In the case of Central Europe, for instance, this would provide much-needed access to the EU market without decontrolling labor migration. Such an arrangement would make sense if Western Europe cannot spare the resources to handle worker immigration on a large scale. Moreover, early admission of Central Europe to the customs union would create export demand and jobs in that part of the world and hence reduce incentives for illegal migration. The European Union's current policy of barring imports of sensitive goods from Central and Eastern Europe may be the worst policy of all because it reduces job creation abroad and encourages migration.

Most Western Europeans are not ready to accept the idea of alternative types of membership, even though the idea is not novel and in fact underpins the discussion of multiple tiers and variable speeds in the context of EMU. Alternative forms of membership might become more acceptable if EU leaders and politicians were more forthright about the comparative costs of partial versus full membership.

Professor Wegner rightly urges Western Europeans to rethink their policy on trade with non-EU members. Here, too, Western European attitudes are seriously stuck in a rut. Europeans, like their American counterparts, tend to see trade and international competition in simplistic terms: imports compete with domestic products for a home market, which is fixed in size. This view neglects the increasing importance of globalized production. Today an intermediate product may be imported to reduce the cost of a final product destined for a third market. Imports of parts may hurt producers of domestic substitutes but help domestic producers of downstream exports. Often, the result is not only net job creation but an improvement in the average quality of jobs.

Similarly, it may make sense to produce technically complex parts and components at home while letting final assembly move offshore if it is relatively labor-intensive and low value-added. This, too, creates more jobs than it destroys and upgrades the average quality of jobs. Western Europeans have barely begun to think in these terms. The traditional view—especially dear to labor unions—is too narrowly focused, but it is driven by the pressure to protect the present jobs of "insiders" at the expense of potential new and better jobs for everybody. This view runs the additional risk of seducing European leaders into the mistaken belief that rich, high-wage countries cannot conduct mutually beneficial trade with poorer, low-wage countries.

The cyclical component of Europe's current economic difficulties will eventually subside, much as it has before, and Europeans will be inclined to forget their structural problems once again. But dealing with the issue cannot be evaded, only postponed. Sooner or later, the trade-offs between alternative types of widening will have to be faced. Much the same can be said for the trade-offs between intra-Union and global trade policy.

Comment

GARY CLYDE HUFBAUER

In mid-1992, the European Community looked reasonably healthy—problems here and there, nothing critical. By mid-1993, the Community acquired a sickly pallor, evoking our sympathies for the prospective Austrian bride. The bad news from Professor Wegner is that the Community is just as sick as it looks. His good news is that, with extreme measures, a cure is possible.

Meeting in Edinburgh in September 1992, the EC heads of state diagnosed the European malaise as weak investment. They offered two main treatments:

■ Reform fiscal policy—first, curtail the drain of public-sector deficits on the pool of European savings; second, cut subsidies to yesterday's industries and increase outlays on tomorrow's infrastructure.

■ Make the European economy more flexible, particularly by reducing rigidities in the labor markets.

Wegner adds a third treatment, with the same pro-investment objective: open EU markets through liberalized trade with Eastern Europe and successful completion of the Uruguay Round.

All in all, these three prescriptions amount to a call for breaking the grip held by the established economic forces of today and giving more

Gary Clyde Hufbauer is Reginald Jones Senior Fellow at the Institute for International Economics.

weight to the promising forces of tomorrow. This is the right prescription, but it is not easy medicine.

European economic distress can be largely traced to rigid labor practices that have escalated the cost of hiring and retaining workers. Differences between US and EU labor markets are well-known and striking:

- Within the European Union, the employment of labor carries a far higher loading of social costs in the form of social security premiums, protection against layoffs, etc.

- Within Europe the public sector plays a leading role in wage settlements (owing to the scope of public employment), and this role has generally been exercised in ways that push up labor costs throughout the economy.

These differences go a long way toward explaining why the Community created very few private-sector jobs in the 1980s, whereas the United States created millions. But the labor market differences also explain why average EC wages rose sharply in the 1980s, much to the delight of those workers who had jobs, whereas US real wages actually declined for many workers, creating an economic backdrop for Clinton's famous campaign slogan, "It's the economy, stupid."

Europe certainly wants faster job growth, and it certainly would like to escape the investment-hindering consequences of current labor practices. But as Wegner reminds us, Europeans are definitely not willing to buy into the US philosophy of labor markets to get these results. My own modest suggestion for this dilemma is that European governments should try offsetting palliatives: for example, the fiscal authorities could relieve firms of the social overhead costs of employing people with identified characteristics that make them look like prime suspects for long-term employment.

Since a large part of public spending in Europe is committed to social safety-net outlays, reducing deficits will be difficult without reforming social policy. Again, as Wegner tells us, there are practical limits. At most, EU governments may be able to trim the fringes of the social safety net. By comparison, it may be slightly less difficult to move public spending away from subsidies to proven money wasters such as agriculture, steel, and shipbuilding and toward promising infrastructure projects. The dinosaurs from "Jurassic Park" will fight to keep their preserves, but the European public may finally be growing skeptical about the care and feeding of these creatures from the past.

One cure to the European illness that was conspicuously left off Wegner's treatment list is monetary ease. Like many European observers, he apparently accepts two tenets of current central-bank doctrine:

- Inflation spikes must be met with sharply higher nominal interest rates—a Zero Inflation Now (ZIN) philosophy.

- Monetary policy should not be deployed to promote negative real interest rates, even when the economy is very sluggish.

In my view, these doctrinal tenets neither sufficiently recognize the inflation-arresting consequences of open international markets nor the disinflationary thrust of labor-saving technology. Be that as it may, it seems to me that European fiscal authorities should consider fiscal palliatives to ease the anti-investment effects of the prevailing tight money bias. For example, interest received on long-term corporate bonds could be made tax-exempt while interest payments remained tax-deductible. In that way, fiscal policy could make every European the legal equivalent of the semimythical tax-evading Belgian dentist, and market forces would point toward lower real interest rates.

But the most promising (if still difficult) treatment was identified by Wegner—namely, a more open EU trade policy. In the current context of redundant capacity, more liberal trade may not on balance do much for *capacity-expanding* investments, since export industries can service new orders with existing plant and equipment. However, even in the gloomy European scene of the mid-1990s, more open markets should prompt *cost-cutting* investment, both in export and in import-competing industries. In turn, this investment should spark a recovery and boost European productivity.

Comment

HELEN B. JUNZ

Although Professor Wegner says he has more questions than answers, his paper does provide a basic central answer: namely, that the appropriate question is not "Europe: what next?" but rather "Europe: what now?" His starting observation is that Europe is in bad shape, a condition that stems not only from a cyclical downturn but also from underlying structural deterioration. This contrasts sharply with the Europe 1992 expectation that the flexibility and robustness of the European economies would be enhanced through increased internal competition and deregulation.

In analyzing the cycles of European integration, Wegner links forward steps with economic upswings, although the seeds of integration may be sown in successive crises. Certainly, economic stagnation in the early 1980s gave rise to Eurosclerosis, which in turn triggered the Single Market Program in 1985—moving from the Single European Act to the ratification of the Treaty of Maastricht and giving impetus to EU expansion across most of the remainder of Europe.

What events sparked the current wave of growth pessimism and defensive thinking about the future? Was it an excessive boom in investment in expectation of the internal market? Or are there more basic reasons? Wegner implicitly argues that the buoyant economic activity in the second half of the 1980s was not accompanied by fundamental reforms. Therefore, Europe did not lay the necessary foundations for a sustained high level of growth. In other words, Eurosclerosis was suc-

Helen B. Junz is Special Trade Representative and Director, International Monetary Fund, Geneva.

ceeded by Eurocomplacency. He suggests that the consequences—a relatively low rate of employment creation accompanied by very high rates of long-term unemployment—now argue for a high-growth strategy, which is defined as annual growth of 3 to 3.5 percent.

This advice is perhaps more easily prescribed than swallowed, particularly since the body politic already seems to have rejected many of the necessary elements. Wegner lists four requirements:

- reduction of bureaucratic and government intervention in investment, including subsidies, and an increase in labor market flexibility;

- moderation of wage increases in order to support an employment-creating growth strategy, combined with measures for worker participation in rising wealth accumulation in the 1990s;

- measures to improve labor quality;

- an EU-wide scheme for infrastructure projects to improve links (e.g., transportation) between Western Europe and the Central and Eastern European countries in transition.

Although necessary, these elements will not be sufficient to achieve the goals postulated by Wegner. In particular, when exploring the link between growth and job creation, he mistakenly dismisses structural labor market problems on the basis of "the strong employment performance of the Community during the high-growth period between 1986 and 1990," when the economy grew at 3.2 percent and employment rose at 1.2 percent per annum. However, he neglects the fact that the major contribution to employment growth during this period came from an increase in public-sector jobs. Therefore, he misses the fundamental point of difference in employment performance between North America, Japan, and the European Community.

Wegner may be right in arguing that the environment of deregulated and flexible labor markets in North America has provided private-sector jobs in part at the cost of low productivity and meager real wage growth. But undoubtedly, maintenance of high total labor costs in the European Union is a major factor in its failure to engender a lasting improvement in job creation. Whereas North America has experienced stagnation in real wages, the decline in EU growth rates has been accompanied by rising real wages. As high EU labor costs in turn reduced employment opportunities, policies to ease the burden on unemployed workers have led to escalating outlays for income support. Consequently, the sharp rise in public-sector deficits is not unrelated to the rigidity both of labor markets and wage performance.

If the wage and labor market structures indeed provide incentives for labor-saving investments, Wegner's active labor market policy—largely consisting of labor quality improvements together with profit-sharing measures—would seem a rather schizophrenic prescription for employment creation. If employers and those progressively rationed out of the labor market have generally borne the cyclical risk, a policy that shares profits but not losses only tends to create another negative wedge in the labor market. Wegner explicitly accepts that the kind of flexibility in North American labor markets is inappropriate for the Union; he looks for a deus ex machina—in this case, external competition—as the engine for a high-growth strategy. His belief that a sea change in the European labor market policies is not possible is rooted in the same thinking that lies behind the difficulties that beset the Uruguay Round; similar arguments are at the base of the Western European tendency to broaden and deepen trade by reducing internal barriers and by accepting new members rather than by inviting global competition.

In sum, Wegner observes that "European integration and trade expansion furnished the locomotive for overall growth in the Community and also provided the base for large improvements in living standards." External trade liberalization—including links with the reforming countries in Eastern and Central Europe—will help recreate the élan present during earlier stages of integration. Marshaling the ability to take advantage of these opportunities presupposes a certain amount of élan itself. The locomotive can pull only a certain amount of deadweight. In a situation where vested interests that powerfully defend the status quo and safety nets—both for workers and for geriatric industries—have become so extensive that they act as disincentives for taxpayers and effective employment and output creation, it may be well to remember that safety nets, by definition, should provide dependable, vital, but temporary support. That is why they are called safety nets and not safety beds. Once safety nets have become too comfortable, they become part of the problem rather than part of the solution.

3

Monetary Arrangements

NIELS THYGESEN

These are difficult times for writing about deepening the monetary arrangements in the European Union. The European Monetary System (EMS), which was to provide a tight framework for the participating currencies underpinned by improved convergence of economic performance and intensified surveillance of nonmonetary policies, has been relaxed through a drastic widening of the margins of allowable fluctuation in early August 1993. The ratification of the Maastricht Treaty establishes much greater scope for deepening monetary arrangements than existed previously. Since the widening of the fluctuation margins, however, most observers have concluded that several of the main economies are not ready to pursue any of the options that are now theoretically possible. Policymakers' attention has shifted to the need to use the additional freedom for national monetary policy offered by the wider fluctuation margins in order to help end the prolonged recession in Europe and, in particular, to check the rise in unemployment. Despite an ambitious timetable, Economic and Monetary Union (EMU), which occupied center stage in the first few months after the signing of the Maastricht Treaty in February 1992, has faded more into the background and is seen by many, including the British prime minister, as largely irrelevant to current policy issues.

Niels Thygesen is Professor of Economics at the University of Copenhagen; he was member of the Delors Committee, 1988–89. In preparing this paper, the author has benefited from extended joint work with Daniel Gros of the Centre for Economic Policy Studies (CEPS) in Brussels and from his participation in a working group on The EMS in Transition, organized for the European Parliament by the Association for Monetary Union in Europe; see Collignon et al. (1993).

The following section discusses the causes of the gradual dissolution of the previously stable EMS witnessed since the summer of 1992. It also looks critically at the analysis, provided in the April 1993 official reports on the crisis of September 1992 and of the subsequent recurrent turmoil in the foreign exchange markets. This discussion is necessary to limit the range of options for future deepening, to be reviewed later. The third section looks at four advantages of the present regime over either a continuation of the past narrow margins or a total suspension of the EMS.[1] Although the author would not subscribe to the verdict of the *Financial Times'* editorial writer (27 September 1993) that "the EC has fallen upon a perfectly sensible exchange rate system," its features are potentially important, redeeming ones that give some hope that the regime adopted *faute de mieux* offers a basis for progress toward EMU. The fourth section reviews this and other options for achieving such progress in the context of stage two, which started on 1 January 1994. The last section puts forth some tentative conclusions.

Lessons of the EMS Widening

An analysis of the scope for deepening of monetary arrangements must necessarily take as its point of departure the drastic widening of the fluctuation margins, which occurred over the weekend of 31 July–1 August 1993. It may seem otiose today to speculate on how the previous EMS might have been rescued, and naive in particular to view the present regime as simply a temporary lapse in the long process of European monetary integration, which developed its first distinguishing features more than two decades ago with the so-called snake, was extended geographically to most EC member states with the launching of the EMS in 1978–79, and was gradually tightened in the course of the 1980s and early 1990s. Yet any paper that tries to address how to move forward must restate why the stable EMS was scrapped.

The academic literature, of which Eichengreen and Wyplosz (1993) is the leading recent example, tends to focus on two possible causes: increasingly visible misalignment of some currencies participating in the EMS and the perception of financial market participants that a number of EC countries would not have the patience, during prolonged recession, to stick with the monetary policies required for maintaining a fixed exchange rate with the Deutsche mark. Growing impatience with high interest rates was certainly evident in the public debate in several participating countries, and the Bundesbank was not prepared to accelerate

---

1. Throughout this chapter the term EMS is used synonymously with the Exchange Rate Mechanism (ERM), which is the main substantive component of the system.

cuts in German short-term rates as long as the inflationary inertia in Germany had not abated more definitively and as long as the growth rate of the money stock continued to hover above the chosen corridor.

The main conclusion hinted at in Eichengreen and Wyplosz is no doubt correct: the relative weight of the two competing hypotheses—which one may label cumulative overvaluation and anticipation of future policy changes—changed between the September 1992 crisis and the relaxation of the remaining EMS in August 1993, which occurred after they wrote their paper. On the former occasion, it was possible to point to at least one country that by all indicators was suffering increasingly from overvaluation: Italy. Over more than five-and-a-half years with an unchanged exchange rate—apart from the technical adjustment in January 1990 when the lira entered the narrow margins—the Italian inflation rate had remained stubbornly above that in the more stable EMS countries. Even as the German inflation rate picked up significantly in 1990–92, the Italian rate never got within one percentage point of this looser target. The degree of overvaluation, according to most estimates, was somewhere around 15 percent. It is therefore not surprising that the lira was the first currency to be attacked and that markets regarded the initial effort at correction by a devaluation of 7 percent as inadequate, prompting only a few days later the departure of the lira from the system.

The cases of the two other important currencies suspected of being candidates for devaluation—pound sterling and the Spanish peseta—were more complex, partly because these currencies had a shorter experience in the EMS, having joined in October 1990 and July 1989, respectively. As regards the pound, the rate at entry chosen by the UK authorities had been too ambitious in the view of many Continental observers—as well as of most UK models of the exchange rate. On the other hand, the United Kingdom had overcome the initial problems of excess inflation with unexpected speed, due more to the early start of recession than to easily identifiable credibility effects of the pound's participation in the EMS. The peseta underwent real appreciation prior to entry, and Spanish inflation continued at a somewhat faster rate than the average for EC countries. On the other hand, Spain had massive capital inflows, a high rate of investment, and relatively rapid productivity growth.

The interpretation of these two performances is accordingly more difficult than that of the Italian case. Whatever the strength of the case for arguing that the pound and the peseta were also overvalued, the first EMS crisis of September 1992 removed the potential elements of overvaluation. Indeed, in the Italian and UK cases, the misalignment was probably overcorrected; few analyses had shown that these two currencies were overvalued to the extent of the 20 percent by which they depreciated shortly after they were set free to float on 17 September 1992. If cases of misalignment remained, these were some of the nine currencies that remained in the EMS and found their competitiveness vis-à-vis important trading partners and competitors sufficiently worsened to cause a significant overall drag on their economies.[2] Yet it was not unreasonable to believe that for those currencies that remained in the EMS after Black Wednesday, currency relationships inside the system were defensible in terms of fundamentals.

The two subsequent realignments—in November of the peseta and, reluctantly, the Portuguese escudo, and in January of the Irish punt—might still be attributed to special factors that had produced elements of misalignment. Spain had only devalued by 5 percent in September, and both market participants and Spanish industrialists felt that had not gone far enough given the exceptionally high level of unemployment in Spain. Furthermore, the spirited defense of the peseta in the fall, including a tightening of impediments to capital outflows and bold use of unusual financial instruments, had not succeeded in containing the pressures. Ireland, with a third of her trade oriented toward the UK market, obviously felt the heat of the sharp fall of sterling more than other countries, and the new Irish government obtained the largest realignment of its central rate in EMS history (10 percent) at the end of January.

As the turmoil in currency markets continued after the Irish devaluation—and even intensified with pressure on the Danish krone and the French franc in early February—it became clear that the second main cause, self-fulfilling speculation, had assumed greater prominence. When countries with their fundamentals in reasonably good order—low inflation, nominal interest rates close to German levels, and no major external imbalance to suggest misalignment within the system—nevertheless are faced with recurrent speculative attacks against their currencies, only market expectations of future changes in policy can explain these pressures. Such expectations were particularly lively around elections and with the associated uncertainty about the continuation of policies; the experience of Ireland and Spain is illustrative. Though this second phenomenon was not absent in the September 1992 crisis and its aftermath, it gained ground as recession deepened in 1992–93. Good past performance and numerous declarations of an intention to maintain stability-oriented policies were no longer enough to preserve exchange-rate stability. Market participants began to ask themselves with increasing frequency how long countries would have the patience to operate a fixed exchange-rate system in view of the need to differentiate monetary policies between countries more sharply than the high degree of uniformity of nominal interest rates permitted.

---

2. Eichengreen and Wyplosz also, no doubt correctly, refer to the Swedish krona and the Finnish markka as examples of overvaluation prior to September 1992. A combination of unfavorable asymmetric shocks and excess inflation in the late 1980s had exposed weaknesses in the economies of Sweden and Finland, which made their unilateral link to the European currency unit (ECU) overambitious.

Both the increasingly rigid EMS of 1987–92 and the idea of developing it into a full monetary union were based on two important premises. First, all participants should share the objective of medium-term stability of prices. Second, the EC countries participating in the tight EMS and, ultimately, in monetary union were on average likely to be subjected to broadly similar disturbances to their economic performance, whether from outside the European Community or from exogenous events within participating countries. While the first premise still holds, the second was called into question by the large, asymmetric shock of German unification. The EMS and the initiative to achieve full monetary unification were designed primarily to jointly absorb shocks that affected all participants in a broadly similar way, as had been the case with the main external shocks in the 1980s: the fluctuations in US macroeconomic policies and in the price of imported energy. In such situations, it can be convincingly argued that leaving countries free to react by adjusting their strategies of accommodation in a competitive and uncoordinated fashion would likely result in outcomes inferior to those achievable through indirect coordination of the EMS. The EMS was not designed to accommodate a major asymmetric shock affecting primarily one of its participants and calling for some realignment of the relative price levels in Germany and in other EMS countries.[3]

It has subsequently become a subject of some controversy whether the EMS could have coped more adequately with this unique and very large shock by agreeing on a revaluation of the Deutsche mark around the time of unification, or more radically by suspending the Deutsche mark from the parity grid for some extended period. The Bundesbank and some German politicians favored the former solution, but most of the other EMS countries, led by France, rejected it because they feared a loss of credibility for their own policy of pegging firmly to the Deutsche mark. In retrospect, the rejection of a realignment may not have been unwise; if it had been used in, say, 1990, the Deutsche mark revaluation would most probably have been modest, both for reasons of tradition and because the size of the shock was initially underestimated. An initial revaluation could then have triggered expectations of more to come, hence putting downward pressure on non–Deutsche mark currencies and failing to ease the interest-rate constraint on them. Floating might have proved a more useful approach, though it might have brought more exchange rate instability than either Germany or its partners would in the end have accepted.

Whatever the merits of these counterfactual scenarios, the EMS persisted with rigid exchange rates for nearly three years after the fall of the Berlin Wall, and real appreciation of the Deutsche mark during that

---

3. For a good discussion of different paradigms for coordination of national economic policies, see Cohen (1993).

period was achieved through a rise in inflation in Germany rather than by revaluation in nominal terms. At the time of this writing, the real exchange rate of the Deutsche mark has risen by 5 percent in effective rate terms globally and by 7 to 8 percent inside the EMS since the start of the rigid EMS in early 1987 (using producer prices of manufactured goods). While there might have been merit in accommodating the need for real appreciation through some upward flexibility for the Deutsche mark from 1990 onward, the case for introducing it had weakened substantially by 1993, when the D-mark began to show signs of overvaluation. Indeed, if the D-mark had been allowed to float upward from the EMS currencies in 1990, it would quite likely have moved down toward the present level or beyond because Germany appears to need some real depreciation in the medium term in order to restore competitiveness and an improved external balance when activity levels recover. A subsequent section takes up the question of whether that would still occur in the wide-margin EMS that has now been set up.

The EMS was correctly designed, in this author's view, not to accommodate asymmetric shocks in general. That would have undermined the credibility of the more rigid version of the system, seen as necessary to prepare for full EMU. The basic approach of the hard EMS and of the EMU process was to coordinate tightly only monetary policy, leaving member states substantial autonomy in national budgetary policy to enable them to absorb country-specific shocks—subject to the proviso that budget deficits and debt be kept moderate. This basically sound assignment was undermined by the reluctance of the German government to finance through taxation a more substantial part of the additional public expenditure unification required. Consequently, inflation picked up more than would have been necessary, pushing the Bundesbank into a tighter monetary stance for an extended period. With high short-term interest rates in Germany still setting the floor for similar rates in other EMS countries, real interest rates in several partner countries with lower inflation than Germany's became unacceptably high, given the prolonged recession. The system also developed the unappealing property that Germany's partners lost the incentive to reduce inflation and inflationary expectations further because progress in these respects would push up real interest rates even higher. Markets were not unjustified in believing that something had to give, even as at least four countries (Netherlands, Belgium, France, and Ireland) succeeded during the spring and summer of 1993 to reduce their nominal short-term interest rates to a level slightly below Germany's.

Must one conclude from this experience that fixed exchange rates were a mistake and—as many comments in the public debate, notably in the United Kingdom, have suggested—that the effort at locking rates permanently had to be scrapped? Such a conclusion would be a mistake for three reasons.

The first relates to the unique nature of the German unification shock, whose unprecedented size is highly unlikely to be equaled in decades. The second reason is that the tensions created were seriously aggravated by policy mistakes in Germany and the very limited readiness of the other EMS countries to regard unification initially as more than a German problem. Given the conditions when it occurred—a large German external surplus amid hopes that unification would make the Community's largest economy into more of a locomotive to pull the economies of other member states as well—the other EMS countries were happy to share in the demand spillovers. They showed little awareness that the long-term political and economic benefits unification conferred on them justified some short-term sacrifices on their part, notably in the form of direct participation in the financing of the process. As it turned out, they became obliged to finance unification indirectly through generally higher interest rates for an extended period. These policy mistakes leave substantial scope for improvement in the framework of full economic and monetary union. Finally, the third reason is that, by hanging on for so long, the EMS countries had retained the valuable option of moving forward toward more complete monetary unification rather than away from it by introducing an unprecedented degree of flexibility into the system. These three reasons support the view that unification's contribution to the EMS relaxation must not be taken as firm evidence of the infeasibility of a system of rigidly fixed exchange rates.

Policymakers themselves contributed to the rejection of the narrow margins. The two official reports on the lessons to be drawn from the disturbances in the foreign exchange markets between September 1992 and April 1993, presented by the Committee of EC Central Bank Governors and the EC Monetary Committee for the May 1993 meeting of the Economic and Financial Council (ECOFIN), stressed the need for making the EMS more rather than less flexible. Much of the discussion in the two reports was devoted to how officials could develop systems that could provide early warning of pressures on the parity grid. For example, the report of the Monetary Committee (1993, para 5.3) states,

> Its procedures should lead to action, when necessary, well in advance of the development of expectations of change in the markets.

The committee of governors' report (1993, section II, 3) offers similar prescriptions:

> The primary purpose of the surveillance of exchange-rate relationships is to function as an early warning system and to bring views closer as regards the sustainability of central rates or the desirability of a timely realignment.

The explicit admission of the need for evaluating sustainability went beyond the 1987 Basel-Nyborg Agreement, which had confined itself to outlining the mechanisms for defending existing parities. Market participants could not be blamed for paying great attention to this admission and the official reports' failure to distinguish between the past, when some participants in the parity grid had arguably moved into unsustainable positions, and the EMS of early or mid-1993, where maxi-realignments had taken place and the remaining participants were priding themselves individually that their currency was not misaligned. Market participants must also have been amused that officials believed themselves capable of identifying misalignments ahead of market anticipations.

The sections in the official reports dealing with short-term defenses in the EMS left a similarly indecisive impression. For example, the Monetary Committee (1993, para 6.3), having underlined that speculation may occasionally build up against the currency of a country in which economic fundamentals are sound, writes:

> When a currency begins to come under attack in spite of good fundamentals or in spite of strong adjustment measures judged appropriate, the Member State affected must demonstrate its strong will to defend its parity through appropriate measures in accordance with the Basel-Nyborg Agreements. The other Member States will determine to which extent and how they can support these efforts through *appropriate voluntary actions* [italics added].

The governors' report (1993, section 3, i) used language in the same vein:

> . . . there cannot be an automatic and mechanistic response to market tensions, involving symmetrical action on the part of the authorities of countries with weak and strong currencies. . . . The Governors do not rule out the possibility of such action taking place on an ad hoc basis, provided that it does not jeopardize the control of domestic monetary conditions in the country issuing the intervention currency. . . .

This heavily guarded language was not apt to convince market participants of any great firmness in the defense of the parity grid.

One might summarize the message of the two reports in the following way: There are two types of errors one may commit in operating a fixed-but-adjustable exchange rate system. The first is to try to defend rates that are becoming unsustainable. The second is to fail to defend rates that are defensible in terms of economic fundamentals. Having committed the first error in some cases in 1992, the officials had by the spring of 1993 become very determined not to repeat it—so much so that they slipped into the second mistake by failing to declare their commitment to the remaining parity grid. The officials would not even have had to choose between the two conceivable basic aims of an exchange rate system: to prevent any misalignments on a continuous basis (which would normally require regular realignments) and to use the exchange rate for nominal anchoring of a country's price level (which may at times

imply some degree of misalignment). That is because, with the currencies left in the EMS, the two views would arguably lead to the same
conclusion: sticking to the existing parity grid and defending it with
collective determination rather than by means of discretionary and voluntary actions by individual participants.

The EC monetary authorities might, even following their ambiguous
statements of April, have been able to defend the narrow margins if
they had acted decisively on an ad hoc basis in the face of the mounting
speculative pressures of the summer. Instead, they chose on the side of
the "weaker" currencies to pursue a policy of reducing interest rates to
levels at or below German rates while beginning to speak of taking over
the anchor function from the Deutsche mark, while on the side of the
Bundesbank, reductions in strategic short-term interest rates were postponed in the light of a cautious interpretation of strictly domestic indicators, notably the broad money supply. Both groups of countries successfully shielded domestic financial markets from the impact of necessary
foreign-exchange interventions. Yet it is well-known that if both inflow
and outflow countries manage to sterilize the bulk of their interventions,
the need to intervene is perpetuated.

Put differently, it became impossible through these choices of strategy
to follow the carefully constructed rules of the Basel-Nyborg agreements,
which had served well on selected earlier occasions. These agreements
foresee judicious use of three short-term instruments in the defense of
the margins: use of fluctuation margins to absorb the initial disturbances;
intramarginal, and ultimately marginal, interventions when these fluctuations become large; and adjustment of short-term interest rate differentials in the appropriate direction when interventions begin to grow
large. Most elements in this graduated and escalating response were
violated in the crisis atmosphere of the summer of 1993, as they had been
in September 1992. Fluctuations inside the margins did not provide much
of an initial buffer, since markets began to interpret movements toward
the margins as a sign of impending realignment rather than as a signal
that a reevaluation of the currency was required due to an increasing
probability of movement back toward the center. Interventions were relied upon too heavily, despite the efficient means of sterilization, and
countries tried to shift the main burden of intervention onto the partner
currency at the opposite side of the margins. Given the need to repurchase
a "weak" currency from the central bank of the "strong" currency country
within three-and-a-half months, the intention of the Basel-Nyborg agreements was clearly not to build up such massive requirements for subsequent settlements that the necessary reversal of private flows began to
look improbable. Finally, appropriate action on interest rates was blocked
by the perceived need in the "weak" currency countries to lower rather
than raise rates and by the reluctance of the Bundesbank to ease monetary
policy to ensure the survival of the system.

Things came to a head at the end of July when the Bundesbank Council failed to lower interest rates to the extent that market participants had expected—and were led to believe on the basis of the brinkmanship of several of the other participating central banks. With the belated introduction of upward flexibility for the Deutsche mark—and for its companion, the guilder—rejected by other participants, the Bundesbank had to resort to more general flexibility. It is regrettable that a final effort to adjust interest rates in the opposite direction in Germany and in the other countries was not made. Such action had in an earlier speculative crisis—early November 1987—successfully dampened tensions in the EMS. In retrospect it seems quite plausible that a similar package could have worked in 1993.

Some observers have said that the events in 1992–93 illustrate a lack of political will to cope constructively and jointly with the tensions in the system. This, however, is not very informative. Rather, the events highlight policymakers' mistakes—in pretending to be able to defend exchange rates that by 1992 had become misaligned, in becoming overanxious not to repeat that mistake when it was no longer the main issue, and, somewhat earlier, in failing to adopt a more comprehensive approach to German unification and to the asymmetric shock it imposed on EMS participants. These mistakes are by now well-understood, and it is possible that they could not have been remedied by even the most imaginative monetary gimmicks—even though that is the thrust of the above discussion. It was disappointing that the participants, having come as far as they had, found it necessary to give up many of the results of a learning process of more than 14 years. The following section reviews some aspects of the present, much looser system, while the subsequent section returns to a discussion of options for resuming a deepening of Europe's monetary arrangements.

Wide Margins: Some Redeeming Features

The decision to widen margins of fluctuation from ±2¼ percent to ±15 percent at first appeared, at least to this author, to have no particular rationale, except that participants in the ECOFIN Council may have wanted to reduce as much as possible the likelihood that they would have to meet again soon to discuss a crisis in the EMS. But on closer reflection, flexibility through wider margins—rather than by more regular realignments, as had been suggested by the official reports some months earlier—confers some advantages. Four come to mind.

The first is the preservation over an extended period of unchanged central rates. This feature may seem uninteresting in view of the wide scope for fluctuation around these rates that the system currently permits. Nevertheless, the survival of the central rates provides a weak form of anchoring, relative to a suspension of the EMS but also relative to a scenario in which the narrow margins of the past had been retained but a realignment had been carried through in the beginning of August. By retaining the central rates, the monetary authorities have indicated their desire that EMS currencies return to this set of exchange rates. This signal led to expectations of appreciation of the "weaker" currencies, which initially floated downward as the margins were broadened, facilitating the lowering of interest rates without a major depreciation of these currencies against the Deutsche mark. By the end of 1993, the Belgian and the French franc had appreciated back into the previous narrow margins, while the Danish krone was only marginally below its lower margin.

The second advantage is the greater ease with which the present floaters—Italy and the United Kingdom—can return to the EMS when they wish to do so. Italy may want to reenter when national elections have taken place, presumably in early 1994. It may not be politically feasible for the United Kingdom to exercise this option, but it will clearly have the opportunity without deemphasizing the recent switch to a low-inflation policy anchored primarily in domestic indicators. If the wide margins become a more permanent feature in the transition to EMU—as could well be the case, for reasons listed below—the United Kingdom may also see political advantages in reentering.

The other side of the coin is that the economic incentives to rejoin are not as compelling as they appeared to be in the period of the rigid EMS, when credibility effects could be presumed to be important. Such effects had in any case disappeared after the turmoil of September 1992 and subsequent events. It seems unlikely that either the two floaters or the remaining EMS participants would have soon contemplated an early return to the EMS that existed between September 1992 and the end of July 1993. The wide margins at least make it possible to bring more of the EC currencies into one framework.

The third and fourth advantages of retaining the central rates but widening the margins are both linked to provisions in the Maastricht Treaty that may have borne some responsibility for destabilizing foreign exchange markets in 1992–93 and for leaving some unnecessary residual doubt about the exchange rate to be used for the transition from the second stage of the EMU process toward full monetary union. The Maastricht Treaty in Article 109(j) sets as one of the entry requirements to the third and final stage that a member state, in order to qualify, must have observed ". . . the *normal* fluctuation margins provided for by the exchange rate mechanism of the EMS for at least two years without devaluing against the currency of any other Member State. . ." [italics added][4]

---

4. Similar wording is used in the separate protocol on the convergence criteria (article 3).

The decision of the ECOFIN Council on 1 August to widen margins to ±15 percent arguably makes these the "normal" margins; the fact that the Deutsche mark and the Dutch guilder chose to preserve narrower margins bilaterally does not modify this conclusion, though it offers a hint of what may be attempted subsequently by other national monetary authorities through bilateral agreements with their German counterparts.

According to this interpretation, the August decision allows member states, when they feel ready to join a full monetary union, to proceed straight from the present wide margins to permanently locked exchange rates at the beginning of the third stage of the EMU process. This would obviously require that the prospective participants' currencies had been fluctuating within a much narrower range than that afforded by the wide margins. The notion that participants could move straight to the locking of rates from a system now regarded as very loose—and even retrogressive compared with the pre-August 1993 EMS—may seem far-fetched, and it will be discussed further in the next section. However, the main point is simply that individual countries or the ECOFIN Council would not necessarily be obliged to formally constrict the margins in order to resume the EMU process, provided, of course, that they refrain from individual actions to derail the process.

If they were to choose the locked-rate route, participants would also circumvent the potentially destabilizing effects of one omission in the Maastricht Treaty. The treaty does not explicitly constrain the ECOFIN Council in its adoption of the starting date of the final stage of "the conversion rates at which their currencies shall be irrevocably fixed and at which rate the ECU shall be substituted for these currencies" [Article 109(l)]. The general assumption has been that the central rates in existence toward the end of the transitional stage would become the conversion rates, but this is not assured, and there has been speculation in the academic literature and among market participants that some form of final realignment could take place at the end of stage two. If such anticipations were to become widespread, participants with suspect currencies may become less able to meet other nominal convergence criteria, with obvious destabilizing implications. Some central bankers clearly are aware of this unsettling possibility, and they have been unable to rule it out in the absence of clear wording in the treaty.

If the wide margins were to continue right through stage two, the transition to stage three would be smoother. Some currencies may then have stabilized inside the margins at rates that do not coincide with the central rate. If so, markets will anticipate that these average market rates will be chosen for conversion, enabling the transition to take place without disruptive discontinuities in market exchange rates. This is one additional element, more remote and of lesser importance than the first, that will tend to make continuation of the wide margins look a bit more attractive than it does at first glance.

The wide margins take into account one important difficulty in managing a lengthy transition toward the past narrow margins: the problem of stabilizing credibly while central rates can still in principle be realigned. The compromise found in the form of ever-tighter management of the EMS does not now look as attractive, relative to the pure regimes of floating and permanently fixed rates, as it did in 1987–92.

It was argued in the previous section that in the summer of 1993 the EMS participants still had the option of tightening up the EMS further and accelerating the EMU process. They took the opposite direction in early August. Even this step confers some benefits, however, as argued in the present section, and it is important not to sacrifice them in an effort to quickly narrow the margins—unless that step were to be accompanied by reforms in the operations of the past EMS to make the system more robust.

Options for Deeper Monetary Integration in Stage Two

The purpose of the present section is to look at the two options: an early return to a reformed EMS and continuation of the present wide margins for an extended period. Both will be evaluated under the assumption that the ambition remains to move toward EMU and to do so within the framework of the Maastricht Treaty—that is, with some member states, preferably a majority, achieving full monetary union in this decade. Reference will be made to the role that the intermediate institution, the European Monetary Institute (EMI), could play in the transition.

It is natural to start with the approach that was until recently considered the only orthodox one: to proceed with a narrow-margined EMS of ±2¼—possibly narrowing the margins further—and taking whatever steps are judged necessary to make the system more robust. In this context, two main steps will be discussed here: further rules of monetary coordination and efforts to limit capital mobility. The latter, however, is raised only to be rapidly dismissed.

Earlier in this paper, an important weakness of the EMS as it operated prior to August 1993 was identified: inadequate commitment to prescriptions for graduated response to pressures on the exchange rate. The Basel-Nyborg agreements foresaw reliance on fluctuations inside the margins, interventions—preferably coordinated before they become mandatory—and changes in short-term interest rates.[5]

The three elements in the short-term defenses need not be changed, but

---

5. The following relies heavily on the author's contribution to Collignon et al. (1993).

the balance between them should. In particular, some mechanism needs to be introduced to assure that interest-rate responses are triggered early in response to external pressures. In principle, the narrower the margins, the stronger the pressure to escalate the responses. Narrow margins have the double effect of signaling a determination to maintain the exchange rate and requiring rapid use of the two other defensive mechanisms.

Since the experiences of 1992–93 have demonstrated that interventions cannot in practice be unlimited, it may be thought that the transition from these to interest rate changes in the graduated series of responses has become more rapid. However, a greater awareness of the limits to interventions merely tempts markets to test the resolve of the national authorities that are trying to defend their currency. Announcing limits to intervention could be outright destabilizing, particularly if the national authority managing the "weak" currency is thought to be unwilling to alter interest rates actively, because the next response has to be a realignment. It would be preferable to design mechanisms that offer central banks incentives to modify interest rates so as to check the need for intervention.

Peter Bofinger (Collignon et al. 1993) and Graham Bishop (1993) recently have formulated two proposals in this spirit. Bofinger's proposal is to suspend for the entire period of stage two the requirement that a debtor central bank repurchase its own currency acquired by the creditor central bank in interventions. At present, repurchase has to be made within three-and-a-half months (extended from two-and-a-half in the Basel-Nyborg agreements), except for the relatively modest amounts under the debtor quotas in the short-term facility. This provision has been central to the functioning of the EMS in the past because a debtor central bank knows that it soon must repurchase its currency. It has to generate a private capital inflow—or the government must borrow—to enable it to do so. This is an incentive to raise interest rates early that would weaken with an extension of the credit period.

The Bofinger proposal would no doubt harden the reluctance of a creditor central bank to intervene at all because of the risk of its being stuck with the increase in reserves and upward pressures on its money stock for a long time. How could it still be obliged to intervene? If the obligation existed, the creditor central bank would have an incentive to give added weight to external pressures in designing its interest rate policy. By swiftly lowering interest rates, the creditor central bank could minimize intervention, which could otherwise become too onerous. But in so doing, it would lose much of its monetary autonomy. The Bofinger scheme would create a more symmetric system than exists today by increasing the pressure on the creditor central banks. Precisely for that reason, its implementation would be resisted by the Bundesbank, as long as the German monetary authorities see themselves as cast permanently in that role—which may, of course, be an unrealistic assumption.

The Bishop scheme favors creditor central banks and is explicitly asymmetric. It foresees that a country that has lost a large amount of reserves through intervention in support of its currency also loses its monetary autonomy. When liabilities corresponding to a certain percentage of the domestic money supply—15 percent of M2, to be specific—have accumulated as reserves of other EMS central banks, the creditors take control of the debtor's monetary policy and presumably raise interest rates or take other measures to restore confidence in its currency. This prospect obviously gives the debtor a strong incentive to take action early of the type that might otherwise be forced upon him later. This approach will appeal to those monetary authorities that see themselves as trendwise creditors, but hardly to the debtors. It may not even appeal to a large creditor central bank because assuming responsibility for another country's monetary policy at a time when political integration is only moderately advanced could become very burdensome for the creditor. It is an advantage in such a framework to have an international institution to oversee policy adjustments and take the political flak—as the International Monetary Fund does in its lending policy—rather than to project an individual foreign central bank into such a visible role. It must remain an open question whether the creditor central bank would accept the task.

Both the Bofinger and the Bishop plans, appealing as they are for their pure logic, are unlikely to enlist sufficient political support. The proposals also make inadequate reference to the emerging multilateral framework, which should become an increasingly significant feature for the next few years as the EMI begins to operate. There is a case for a third approach that remedies these weaknesses by combining the best elements of the two plans.

One element in the September 1992 crisis was that both strong- and weak-currency countries strongly resisted drawing the money-supply and interest-rate implications required for interventions to achieve stability. The Bundesbank prided itself on having proved able to sterilize 90 percent of the interventions undertaken within a short period. Some of the weak-currency countries made a similar effort to sterilize fully; it is difficult, for example, to see any trace of the dramatic outflow from the United Kingdom in the monthly UK money supply figures for 1992.

It is a well-known property of a fixed exchange rate system that the higher the degree of combined sterilization of interventions, the more unstable the system becomes. If all participants succeed in sterilizing completely, stability would hinge only on the so-called portfolio effect: as additional volumes of financial assets denominated in the weak currency are held reluctantly, an increasing premium return is required, which dampens activity in the deficit country and conversely in the surplus country. Empirical work by Dominguez and Frankel (1993) and others suggests that this effect is modest, because even in turbulent periods interventions are small relative to the total stocks of financial assets denominated in the respective currencies. Nearly fully sterilized interventions will therefore continue for a long time because they reduce only marginally the tensions that prompted them.

This is the problem the Bofinger and Bishop proposals address, though in ways likely to meet maximum resistance. If repurchase obligations for the deficit country were to be suspended for a lengthy period, as proposed by Bofinger, sterilization would become harder in the longer term for the surplus country, which is accordingly likely to resist by intervening less and by trying to push the burden of adjustment back onto the deficit country. If monetary autonomy is lost by the deficit country automatically once it has lost an important part of its reserves, the deficit country may resort too quickly to the instrument it can control: devaluation.

A more acceptable device might be one in which sterilization practices in both the surplus and the deficit country are monitored collectively on a continuing, short-term basis. After 1 January 1994, the EMI could manage collective action. Its potential for discharging such a task would be enhanced if a significant number of participating national central banks were to use the provisions of the Maastricht Treaty (Article 6.4) to entrust to the EMI the task of managing their foreign exchange reserves, in which case the EMI would undertake the interventions. No specific norms would be set for the degree of sterilization; discretionary judgments would be made from day to day as to whether the need for intervention was accelerating, in which case the degree of sterilization would be reduced, or decelerating, and no change in recent practice would be required. The scheme would be designed to speed up the transition from sterilized to nonsterilized interventions in circumstances where the gradualist approach of Basel-Nyborg is blocked and a risk is perceived that the deficit country will be tempted or forced into a devaluation not warranted by fundamentals.

The proposed scheme would be facilitated if the EMI were also empowered through bilateral contracts to manage domestic money market operations of the participating central banks. Such a pooling of operations was suggested during the work of the Delors Committee by Professor Alexandre Lamfalussy (who has recently been appointed president of the EMI) in order to make all operations by each central bank more transparent to other participants while presenting a more common front to market participants. In the Lamfalussy proposal, only operations were to be pooled; no transfer of decision-making authority was to take place. The proposal did not meet with favor among the national central bankers—somewhat surprisingly, since it was a minimalist proposal that could nevertheless have improved the efficiency of the operations, and not only in an international sense. Preoccupied as the discussion was with the detailed blueprint for ultimate monetary union, with a European system of central banks combining central decision making with decentralized implementation of policy, the idea of early centralization of operations did not fit in very well. The experience of the 1992 currency crisis justifies a reconsideration of this reluctance. But in order to prevent speculative attacks from succeeding when they are basically seen as unwarranted, some pooling of authority would now be required.

As in the case of the proposals by Bofinger and Bishop, the present proposal will be challenged on the grounds that monetary sovereignty is transferred to an unacceptable degree. The following section takes up briefly the limits of the principle of indivisibility of monetary policy.

As the Delors Committee did its work, the most difficult task was to define how the transition to monetary union was to take place. It was obvious that the starting point in the EMS was one in which monetary authority rested ultimately in national hands. The EMS is a system of rules relying in the end on the willingness of independent states to let their central banks cooperate. The incentives for them to do so were becoming visibly stronger in the 1980s, as economic performances began to converge and capital controls were removed. But the mere fact that realignments could occur made it obvious that in the end there was an escape route. The lack of central bank autonomy in several member states increased the likelihood that policy conflicts between countries would escalate quickly to the political level and create public debate, which would encourage market expectations that the system was becoming vulnerable. For a long time prior to the 1992 crisis, these two elements receded into the background, and central bank publications offered the rosy picture that voluntary monetary cooperation was quite adequate to the task. Many central bankers would have preferred to leave matters like that and to adopt a very slow gradualist approach to monetary integration. They feared that forcing a speedy pace toward monetary union would stir up political antagonisms, putting their regular task of managing the EMS at risk.

The European Council in 1988 asked the Delors Committee, comprising largely central bank governors, to study how EMU could be realized and to propose concrete stages leading toward this objective. In meeting the former of these challenges, the committee outlined an advanced form of monetary unification with a federal central banking institution, issuing a single currency as soon as possible after the definitive locking of intraunion exchange rates. Bini-Smaghi, Padoa-Schioppa, and Papadia (1993) have aptly termed the inspiration for this blueprint of monetary union "national," in the sense that monetary policy in the union would have to be designed as it is in large individual countries rather than as an advanced form of international policy coordination. All monetary conflicts would be fully internalized inside the union.

This was clearly a system qualitatively different from the existing EMS, even compared with an optimistic assessment of the state of monetary integration at the end of the 1980s. Accordingly, there was a long road to travel to the final stage, and it is obvious from the nature of the proposals that the central bankers initially assumed that the transition would also take a long span of years. As the subsequent political debate developed during negotiations on the Maastricht Treaty, which set dates not too far into the future, the vagueness and fragility of the preparations for the transition stood out even more clearly than before. Paradoxically, the more the transition deadlines were telescoped, the less substantial the concrete provisions for transition became. Symbolically, the European Central Bank was no longer to begin in stage two with the transition from coordination of independent national monetary policies to the formulation and implementation of a common policy in the final stage. Instead, there was only a temporary and preparatory EMI, which looks like a slightly modified Committee of Central Bank Governors.

Yet several of its features would tend to give the EMI a higher profile publicly and greater authority as a mediator/coordinator for the central banks than that enjoyed by the committee: the nomination by the European Council of a full-time EMI president, the requirement that the members of its council exercise their collective functions without receiving political instructions, the capacity of the council to make recommendations on the conduct of monetary policy in the member states, the possibility that national central banks will delegate some of their tasks to the new institution, and above all, the intended preoccupation of the EMI with planning for policy in the final stage. But it is clear that de jure there will be very little the EMI can do to impose its authority. It will have to rely on persuasion.

Is it possible to envisage a transition in which monetary authority is somehow shared between the national level and EMI? The Delors Committee deliberated long on this issue, but efforts to develop specific proposals under the heading of "gradualism and indivisibility" had to be given up—not only because there was disagreement on substance, but also because any precise description of a division of responsibilities during the transition would have been very difficult to draw up. Obviously, there should be no doubt in financial markets as to who is responsible for any particular decision, but would that necessarily preclude the attribution of some clearly defined policy functions to the EMI? Could, for example, as was proposed by some members of the Delors Committee, two important instruments of monetary management—one external, interventions in third currencies, and one "domestic," changes in Europewide reserve requirements—be assigned to the EMI while leaving other instruments in national hands?

It is tempting to argue the case for such a division of responsibilities, but by now it would be rather unproductive. The Germans—and some others—have indicated their firm opposition to any intermediate stage between the decentralized framework of the present and the federal model of the final stage. Nothing can change that as a practical reality. But still, the environment within which policymaking nationally or collectively takes place can be modified in ways that shift the incentive for voluntary coordination strongly toward collective action and management so that the system de facto begins to operate as a closer substitute for a common monetary policy.

Two changes in the environment appear central. The first, which is already occurring, is to make the national central banks more independent of their respective governments. This will at the same time make them more dependent on each other. In Maastricht it was argued that initiatives of this kind should be delayed until the final days of the transition to EMU. But since then, several modifications in the status of the central banks have occurred or are under way, most significantly in France. The risk that incipient policy conflicts would quickly escalate to the political level has in the past severely constrained voluntary central bank cooperation in the EMS. The most dramatic event in the 1992 crisis was the public policy conflict between the Bundesbank and the British Treasury.

The second change in the environment for central bank cooperation would come about as the EMS becomes more symmetric. When the decision to fully dismantle capital controls was made in 1988, the challenge of near-complete capital mobility prompted reflections on how to share monetary policy more efficiently in the long term and pushed the monetary authorities into tighter cooperation. Notably, interest rate convergence became stronger than in the past. Leadership in monetary policy began to be more widely shared among the participants as the relative financial weight of Germany declined. But this process was reversed by the shock of German unification and the exceptional need for the Bundesbank to maintain high interest rates in its aftermath. Leadership shifted back to Germany, not because it had a superior economic performance, as in the mid-1980s, but because of the need to conduct the tightest monetary policy in the European Community.

This phase now appears to be coming to an end. As German interest rates decline in recession and German stability is no longer superior to that of several other member states, the anchor function will widen to comprise all the countries conducting stable, noninflationary policies— whether this development is planned or not. Germany will obviously continue to exercise the influence its financial weight accords it, but at a diminished level. In this process, the German attitude toward tighter forms of monetary cooperation should change, and the limits of the doctrine of indivisibility of monetary policy should be explored. As financial markets change their evaluation of Germany's economic prospects, Germany will see its own interest in testing new initiatives and procedures such as those advocated in the previous section for sharing monetary sovereignty. The growing independence of the central banks of partner EMS countries will be a major determinant of the speed with which these changes will occur. Other countries are now showing their capacity for anticipating this new opportunity.

All the above discussion has taken as a starting point the premise that a clear majority of EMS countries will wish to return soon to narrow margins and the familiar territory of the previous EMS, perhaps in the course of 1994. This chapter has focused on ways the system could then be made more robust: more monetary coordination, blurring the principle of indivisibility of monetary policy during the transition, and imaginative use of the potential operational and advisory role (with added authority) of the EMI.

The discussion did not take up one idea that has received much attention in some academic circles (mainly in the United States) and in some official circles in Europe—that is, to attempt to dampen the incentive for short-run capital movements through a tax on all foreign exchange transactions (a "Tobin tax") or an obligatory non–interest bearing deposit at the central bank against the open foreign exchange position of private banks within its jurisdiction.[6] Such steps could be seen as a way of making speculation more costly, while giving the national authorities time to better organize their defense of the exchange rate in times of crisis.

This omission is deliberate; if this approach were indeed seen as a necessary condition for reverting to a narrow-margined EMS, the latter would be premature. The inefficiencies introduced by such schemes are well-known and are recognized even by their advocates. Their usefulness, even in the short run, depends on universal application within the European Union, at a minimum; restricting their application to some EMS countries would be both ineffective and inappropriate for an area that is attempting to retrieve rapid and deep financial integration. There is little point in trying to block or punish speculators. What is needed is to create an environment in which there is no scope for wasteful speculation when the fundamentals are in good order but where scope remains for welfare-enhancing hedging on the rare occasions when they are not. Subjecting national policies to market judgment was one important purpose of the Community's lifting of capital controls in recent years, and the convergence criteria in the Maastricht Treaty were designed to give market participants some indicators to watch—that is, those criteria that governments regarded as central in assessing member states' credentials for eventual participation in full monetary union. Positive interaction with market participants should not be impeded, but mechanisms to defend exchange rates in cases where the fundamentals

6. For a discussion of these ideas, see Eichengreen and Wyplosz (1993).

are judged to be in good order should be strengthened along the lines outlined above.

Let us now consider an alternative scenario in which the present wide margins are retained for an extended period and no effort to narrow margins is attempted because of fears of repeating the experience of 1992–93.

There are two versions of this alternative scenario: one pessimistic or alarming, the other quite smooth. Under the former, political impatience with recession mounts in the short term to such an extent that one important country (or several member states) embark on aggressive policies of sharply cutting short-term interest rates. Since the effects of more expansionary monetary policies are slow to show up in output and employment gains, pressures may build to proceed more aggressively along the path chosen. An acceleration of interest rate cuts and/or of expansionary budgetary policies will lead to significant movements among EMS currencies as the wider margins are tested, to unwarranted further appreciation of the Deutsche mark, and to a deteriorating climate for European integration, with mutual recriminations about competitive devaluations. The construction of the internal market in the European Union cannot be assumed to be immune to a significant increase in currency instability among participants. Member countries will have traded some perceived short-term gains for major long-term costs; in this scenario it will not be feasible to resume progress toward EMU by narrowing margins or by other initiatives for a long time to come.

Fortunately, this pessimistic scenario seems increasingly unlikely, though this verdict is tentative. Initially, because of the need to maintain interest rates high enough to encourage capital flows back into countries with depreciated currencies and the desire to make speculation costly, most weak-currency countries have not behaved very differently than they would have under the previous system. Eventually they will, though by that time German interest rates will have been reduced, dampening major exchange rate fluctuations. As the temporary depreciation of the Deutsche mark focuses the attention of more market participants on the weakness of Germany's competitive position and the need to correct it through such depreciation, there will be scope for further, though cautious cuts in non-German short-term interest rates without risking major currency instability. The general easing of monetary policy will directly reduce the interest part of public-sector deficits and indirectly make some budget consolidation feasible, in correspondence with the convergence criteria.

Assume, for the sake of argument, that after an initial 6 to 12 months of some volatility, exchange rates inside the wide margins begin to stabilize at levels not very different from those prevailing before August. If member states remain committed to the nominal convergence criteria and adopt similar inflation targets for their individual economies—say, about 2 percent for 1995–96—there would be a limit as to how far apart their currencies and long-term interest rates could drift. In this version of the scenario, member states would have the option of narrowing the margins very significantly—back to ±2¼ percent or something even tighter. This author's preference would be that they then take that option, provided they are prepared to take some visible steps to make the system more robust than in the past, along the lines suggested above. The likelihood that it will then be less obvious whether there are any trend-wise creditors or debtors in the system should make proposals to effectively pool some monetary authority in the EMI more palatable. Above all, participants will be able to claim that the exchange rate constellation that has emerged in the markets has a higher degree of credibility than the previous politically determined structure underpinned by occasionally large-scale interventions and that it therefore merits renewed confirmation in a narrow-margin arrangement.

While this could seem to be the best outcome, it may be that the memories of 1992–93 are still too fresh and the performance of the more flexible system sufficiently smooth to persuade policymakers to persist with the wide margins and avoid another ignominious retreat from an arrangement where rates are in principle fixed but realignments cannot in practice be excluded prior to full monetary union. The previous section argued that governments would be under no obligation to adopt narrow margins in order to return to the path toward EMU. They could, in principle, retain that option by sticking to their convergence criteria with greater determination. The inflation and interest rate criteria appear presently quite manageable for more than a majority of member states, but the budgetary criterion—leaving aside the reference value for debt levels, widely recognized to be unrealistic but fortunately also superfluous—will need to receive more serious attention. That will become possible as interest rates decline, the unbalanced policy mix is somewhat corrected, and modest output growth resumes. With budget deficits falling more or less in parallel from the present average level of about 6½ percent of GDP in the European Union to below 5 percent by 1995–96, one can reasonably forecast that a first effort to determine whether a majority of member states are ready for full EMU could reach a positive verdict, and within the time scale foreseen in the Maastricht Treaty—that is, before the end of 1996.

Even in the scenario in which the wide margins are retained up to that point—for three years or so—it may therefore be quite feasible to achieve full EMU according to Maastricht principles and timetable, although the route will be rather different from that envisaged by the treaty's drafters. In particular, the transition would put more emphasis on direct policy coordination and on the readiness of member states to meet the convergence requirements and obviously less emphasis on exchange rate management, which has been the fulcrum of policy efforts in the past.

Conclusions

This paper has looked at the causes of the dramatic tensions in the previous EMS since summer 1992. For a system that always claimed to emphasize fundamentals as determinants of exchange rates, 1992–93 brought a double defeat. In September 1992 the monetary authorities felt obliged to give up defending some currencies for which fundamentals should have been recognized as being askew. With these misalignments removed, the remaining monetary authorities chose to give up the defense of rates that by the system's own criteria should have been defended. These experiences suggest that if there is a move back to narrow margins, the system needs to be reinforced by tighter coordination of monetary policy and EMI surveillance.

The very wide margins now in existence are regrettable and serve as an example of failure in policy coordination. Nevertheless, they have brought relief, and there are some redeeming features. The most important ones may be those that reduce the risk of instability inherent in the provisions of the Maastricht Treaty for transition and for conversion rates for currencies participating in full EMU, to be set at the end of stage two.

Two main options have been discussed. In the first, member states move back to narrow margins after a fairly short period and implement several reinforcements of the EMS that imply some pooling of monetary authority in stage two. In the second, member states retain the wide margins throughout the transition and focus on nearly complete convergence of nominal variables and considerable budgetary consolidation, all through their individual efforts and with EMI surveillance. Though the first scenario is the author's preferred one, both could lead to full EMU for a significant majority of member states within the time frame foreseen in the Maastricht Treaty. Given the experience of tensions in the EMS and the system's partial suspension, the second route may now appear the safer one.

References

Bini-Smaghi, Lorenzo, Tommaso Padoa-Schioppa, and Francesco Papadia. 1993. "The Policy History of the Maastricht Treaty." Paper presented at a conference on The Monetary Future of Europe, organized by the Centre of Economic Policy Research in la Coruna, Spain, Banca d'Italia (February).

Bishop, Graham. 1993. "Is There a Rapid Route to an EMU of the Few?" *Economic and Market Analysis* (11 May). London: Solomon Brothers. Also published in Templeton (1993).

Cohen, Daniel. 1993. "Coordination across the Atlantic and across the Rhine." Paper presented at a conference on The Future of the International Monetary System, organized by the International Center for Monetary and Banking Studies, Geneva (September).

Collignon, Stefan, with Peter Bofinger, Christopher Johnson, and Bertrand de Maigret. 1993. *The EMS in Transition*. A study prepared for the European Parliament, Association for the Monetary Union of Europe, Paris (July).

Committee of Governors of the Central Banks of the Member States of the European Community. 1993. "The Implications and Lessons to be Drawn from the Recent Exchange Rate Crisis." Basel (21 April).

Dominguez, Kathryn M., and Frankel, Jeffrey A. 1993. *Does Foreign-Exchange Intervention Work?* Washington: Institute for International Economics.

Eichengreen, Barry, and Wyplosz, Charles. 1993. "The Unstable EMS." *Brookings Papers on Economic Activity* 1993: 1, 51–143. Washington: Brookings Institution.

Fratianni, Michele, Juergen van Hagen, and Christopher Waller. 1992. "The Maastricht Way to EMU." *Princeton Essays in International Finance* no. 187 (June). Princeton, NJ: International Finance Section, Princeton University.

Gros, Daniel, and Thygesen, Niels. 1992. *European Monetary Integration: From the European Monetary System to European Monetary Union*. London: Longman.

Kenen, Peter B. 1992. *EMU after Maastricht*. Washington: Group of Thirty.

Lamfalussy, Alexandre. 1989. "A Proposal for Stage Two Under Which Monetary Policy Operations Would Be Centralised in a Jointly-Owned Subsidiary." Collection of papers annexed to the *Delors Report*. Luxembourg: Office of Publications of the European Community.

Monetary Committee of the European Community. 1993. "Lessons to Be Drawn from the Disturbances on the Foreign Exchange Markets." Brussels (13 April).

Pisani-Ferry, Jean, Michel Aglietta, and Agnes Benassy. 1993. "Nouveau SME: La règle du jeu." *La Lettre du CEPII* No. 116 (September). Paris: Centre d'Études Prospectives et d'Informations Internationales.

Templeton, Paul, ed. 1993. *The European Currency Crisis*. Cambridge: Probus Publishing Company.

Comment

PETER B. KENEN

My remarks will track closely the organization of Niels Thygesen's paper. I will start with the lessons to be learned from the monetary crises of 1992 and 1993, turn next to the problem of deepening monetary cooperation in stage two of EMU, and end with some thoughts on the evolution of the EMS. I will assume, as does Thygesen, that the governments of the European Union are still committed to the aims of the Maastricht Treaty, though some of them have doubts about certain provisions or deadlines.

Thygesen's paper makes a useful contribution to the debate about ways to move ahead with EMU, and I agree with much of it. But I must stress three matters on which we disagree.

First, Thygesen's interpretation of recent history is rather Panglossian. He seems to believe that all has been for the best in this second-best of all possible worlds.

Second, Thygesen is too optimistic about prospects for deepening monetary cooperation in stage two and, more important, wrong in stressing the need to shift responsibility for the execution of monetary policy rather than stressing the need to limit autonomy in the choice of national policy targets.

Third, Thygesen may attach too much importance to achieving exchange rate stability in stage two and to the eventual narrowing of the exchange rate band.

Peter B. Kenen is Walker Professor of Economics and International Finance and Director of the International Finance Section at Princeton University.

Interpreting Recent History

I do not disagree with Thygesen's chief point about the recent crises, which he in turn ascribes to Eichengreen and Wyplosz (1993), that a fundamental misalignment of exchange rates played a key role in triggering the 1992 crisis but that short-term policy dilemmas played the key role in triggering the 1993 crisis. I would thus agree with his conclusion that the 1992 crisis had a therapeutic value because it corrected the misalignment. But this difference between the two crises is less important in my view than their basic similarity.

What happened in September 1992? Did foreign exchange markets come suddenly to realize that the lira and pound were overvalued? No. They came to realize that the Maastricht Treaty was in trouble because of the Danish and French referendums and equally deep disaffection in other EU countries and that the convergence criteria were therefore in trouble. Without the discipline imposed by those criteria, moreover, Italy might be unable to mimic German monetary policy in the face of deep domestic recessions. In other words, both crises were from the start credibility crises that cast doubt on the ability of the EU countries to keep their exchange rates fixed during the long transition to EMU. And when such doubts arise about the medium-term outlook, they usually trigger market responses that telescope them quickly into doubts about the short-term outlook. In this general sense, the 1992 crisis, no less than the 1993 crisis, was a serious setback for EMU.

Furthermore, the first credibility crisis led us to look back at the treaty itself and note that the long transition to EMU could easily produce many similar episodes—occasions on which a particular country's situation would be called into question. What will happen, we asked, in the weeks and days before the Council of Ministers is obliged to declare that Greece, Italy, or Belgium is running an excessive budget deficit? In short, we came to understand that stage two of EMU is accident-prone and may be unworkable unless it is made more robust. I will return to this matter.

I have other problems with Thygesen's assessment of recent history. I do not know what the Bundesbank would have done if the Deutsche mark had been revalued in 1990 or 1991. It might have pursued a tight monetary policy, even if there had been less inflation in Germany, to signal the need for fiscal and wage restraint and slow the growth of the money supply. Nevertheless, the expenditure-switching effects of a German revaluation would have made it easier for other EU countries to tolerate high interest rates had they been forced to follow the Bundesbank. Thygesen's views of this issue are all the more puzzling in light of his assertion that the EMS was not meant to deal with a large asymmetrical shock in Europe. I am likewise puzzled by Thygesen's silence on another matter—how anyone could have believed that the exchange-rate and interest-rate changes made by Italy and Germany on 14 September 1992, just before the lira left the ERM, were big enough to reassure foreign exchange markets. Large mistakes were made and must be acknowledged. Otherwise, they may be repeated.

There are other instances in which Thygesen rewrites history. He says, for example, that the rigid version of the EMS was "seen as necessary to prepare for full EMU." This turns history upside down. It was EMU that was seen as necessary to supplant the rigid EMS because the latter was seen to be fragile. Remember the argument made at the time, most notably by Padoa-Schioppa (1988), that the EMS would be vulnerable after the lifting of capital controls unless its members adopted a single monetary policy—and they could not do that for long unless it was a European monetary policy. And Thygesen-as-Pangloss goes much too far when he praises the last-ditch defense of the rigid EMS for giving its members "the option of moving forward" by "introducing an unprecedented degree of flexibility in the system." If this was such a good idea, why wasn't it adopted earlier?

I have similar problems with Thygesen's interpretation of the Basel-Nyborg agreement but will not take time to recite them.

Monetary Cooperation in Stage Two

What can be done to make stage two more robust? Thygesen makes intriguing recommendations, and though I have questions about them, his proposals deserve serious consideration.

Thygesen seeks to transform the EMI into an important actor. He would give it control over certain instruments of monetary policy, the right to decide—or at least recommend—that central banks should not sterilize their interventions on foreign exchange markets, and the power to conduct intervention on its own. In effect, he seeks to rehabilitate the proposal made by the Delors report, that stage two should involve a gradual transfer of responsibility for monetary policy, without explicitly challenging the "indivisibility" of that responsibility.

This strategy, however, will not deceive anyone, least of all those who insist on the principle of indivisibility. The EMI cannot manipulate any policy instrument without first having a policy target. Any such target, moreover, must be European, not national, in domain. To be specific, the EMI would have to pursue price stability in the European Union as a whole, and the policy stance appropriate for that purpose will not always coincide with the one appropriate for price stability in each country individually. The pursuit of price stability in France, for example, would not have required the stringent monetary policy that Germany needed after 1990.

One can perhaps conceive of an arrangement under which the EMI would use one policy instrument to pursue price stability in the European Union as a whole and each of the national central banks would use some other instrument to differentiate its own monetary policy from that of the EMI. Any such arrangement, however, is more likely to produce recrimination than finely tuned differentiation.

There is another difficulty. Recall Article 12 of the European Central Bank (ECB) statute, which says in part:

> To the extent deemed possible and appropriate . . ., the ECB shall have recourse to the national central banks to carry out operations which form part of the tasks of the ESCB.

Some would say that this clause was meant merely to appease the national central banks. I have argued elsewhere, moreover, that the conduct of a single monetary policy will require institutional innovations that will deprive the clause of any economic significance. There will be the need, in particular, for a single, ECU-denominated interbank market, analogous to the federal funds market in the United States, and once that market starts to function, there will be no real need for the ECB to delegate or distribute its operations. At the start of stage three, however, the links between each country's banking system and its own national central bank may still differ importantly from country to country, and the ECB may have to make meaningful use of the national central banks to implement its policies (see Kenen 1992; Monticelli and Viñals 1993). The point applies with greater force to conditions in stage two. One cannot authorize the EMI to adjust reserve requirements without first introducing and aligning them in every EU country. It would be even harder for the EMI to conduct open-market or credit operations. What assets would it hold and use?

Thygesen's second suggestion, that there be a partial pooling of reserves in the EMI, allowing it to intervene in foreign exchange markets, has been made before, but there are two difficulties. First, the EMI is not authorized to intervene but merely to "hold and manage reserves as an agent for and at the request of national central banks." Furthermore, it must follow rules designed to make sure that its transactions "shall not interfere with the monetary policy and exchange rate policy of the competent monetary authority of any Member State . . ." (Article 6.4 of the EMI statute). It should be noted, moreover, that the EMI cannot really pool reserves. If Italy deposited Deutsche marks with the EMI, they could presumably be used to buy lira. But could they be used to buy Spanish peseta without the consent of the Italian authorities?

Which brings us to another, more serious matter. When deciding whether the EMI should be given a large role in managing EMS exchange rates, one must ask whether the EMI would have access to the short-term credit facilities of the EMS, directly or *via* the central banks whose currencies it was supporting. Otherwise, a delegation of responsibility to the EMI might actually reduce the stock of resources available for intervention.

The Evolution of the Exchange Rate Regime

My comments on the EMI should not be misinterpreted. I share Thygesen's basic objective, the deepening of monetary cooperation in stage two of EMU. I have reservations, however, about the approach he proposes— an attempt to transfer instruments or operations to the EMI in the tacit hope that this will compel the national governments and central banks to reach agreement on the objectives it should pursue. I am therefore pessimistic about prospects for deepening cooperation, which leads me to my last point.

If I am right to be pessimistic and equally right to say that stage two will be accident-prone, it would be extremely unwise to move back to very narrow bands at any time before the final locking of exchange rates, which will of course banish the bands completely. I do not believe it was necessary to widen the bands all the way to 15 percent in August, and I do not believe it will be necessary keep them that wide throughout stage two. In fact, it might be wrong to do so because very wide bands will leave too much room for exchange rates to deviate from their central rates and may thus create controversy, as well as uncertainty, about the rates that will be locked at the beginning of stage three. Should they be the central rates or the prevailing market rates?

Let me make a suggestion that will convey my own views about the exchange rate regime for stage two. On 1 January 1994, the countries participating in the exchange rate mechanism should make three statements.

First, they should reduce the bands from 15 percent to, say, 7½ percent.

Second, they should reformulate the conclusion reached in the reports of the Monetary Committee and the Committee of Central Bank Governors. Realignments may be needed and are likely to occur in the first years of stage two, but they will not be larger than the width of the new band.

Third, the countries should say that the locking of exchange rates, if it occurs on 1 January 1997, will take place at the central rates prevailing on 30 June 1996. This is, of course, a way to signal there will be no realignments in the six months before the decision about starting stage three.

What should they say if stage three does not start on 1 January 1997? They need not say anything. They will be exposed to severe exchange market pressures if the decision is deferred, no matter what they say, but can fend off those pressures more easily if they stay with 7½ percent bands than by moving back to the old 2½ percent bands.

References

Eichengreen, Barry, and Charles Wyplosz. 1993. "The Unstable EMS." *Brookings Papers on Economic Activity* 1.

Kenen, Peter B. 1992. *EMU After Maastricht.* Washington: The Group of Thirty.

Monticelli, Carlo, and José Viñals. 1993. "European Monetary Policy in Stage Three: What Are the Issues?" In G. de la Dehesa et al., *The Monetary Future of Europe.* London: Centre for Economic Policy Research.

Padoa-Schioppa, Tommaso. 1988. "The European Monetary System: A Long-Term View." In F. Giavazzi, S. Micossi, and M. Miller, *The European Monetary System.* London and New York: Cambridge University Press.

Comment

MASSIMO RUSSO

Professor Thygesen has given a relatively optimistic view of where monetary cooperation and integration in the European Union could be going. Even so, we are far from the Maastricht euphoria of late 1991 and the first half of 1992.

Our friends across the Atlantic, I am sure, will think that no optimism is justified or warranted; floating is the "natural" state. This we also see in the IMF Executive Board: it seems the further you are from Europe, the more you stress floating.

The lessons to draw from the exchange rate crisis in Europe in 1992–93 must be based on the following five points:

- The EMS has served a very important purpose for almost a decade and a half; it is equally important now to build constructively on this experience.

- The single market cannot survive the real exchange rate swings and persistent misalignments that have characterized relations among the G-3 currencies.

- A new attempt therefore will be made to limit exchange rate flexibility in the European Union. In this sense, the solution adopted on 1 August 1993 to maintain prevailing central rates and fix an admittedly wide band for fluctuations is useful, as Thygesen correctly points out.

Massimo Russo is Director, European I Department, International Monetary Fund.

- The shock of German unification was unprecedented for its size, concentration, *and because it involved the anchor currency*; this is unlikely to be repeated (though other shocks can occur; just look east of Vienna!).

- The expansion and integration of capital markets will continue to intensify, and no country that pretends to be an international financial center will be prepared to reestablish controls on international capital movements.

Reconstruction should be based on the Maastricht Treaty (a new negotiation is unthinkable), without the pitfalls of its insistence, simultaneously, on deadlines and conditions, which, coupled with too narrow margins, invite speculative attacks. Decisions concerning exchange rates and monetary policy cannot be treated the same way as those that involved customs duties and other nontariff barriers and rules.

As I see them, the crucial questions are:

- Should the Deutsche mark remain the only anchor until the move into EMU?

- Can effective monetary cooperation gradually develop into a common monetary policy?

- While exchange rates are allowed to move within wider margins, can convergence be achieved and sustained?

Arrangements such as those between the Netherlands and Austria and Germany are sustainable and have not been seriously questioned by markets. The situation, however, is different for the larger countries, making the need for monetary cooperation essential. But this remains incompatible with the mandate of the Bundesbank.

It is too early to answer these difficult questions. In any case, Germany must first right its imbalances before a stable regime can be reconstructed. The last scenario of Thygesen's, wherein exchange rates are stabilized through convergence and monetary coordination within the existing wide margins, is the most likely route to EMU and in my view a desirable one. It will confirm which country can sustainably maintain low inflation and resolve the discontinuity between adjustable and permanently fixed exchange rates. It implies a two-speed Europe on its road to EMU, but this is in the Maastricht Treaty.

While there are similarities between the demise of the Bretton Woods system and the EMS, there is also a major difference. Under the dollar standard, Germany and Japan resorted to floating because they did not want to import the higher US inflation. The EMS fell upon exactly the opposite conflict: restrictive German monetary policies imposed deflation on the partners. Once Germany has returned durably to a low-inflation path and the Bundesbank has eased monetary policy further, this conflict will have been solved. The move to EMU, requires, however, that other structural issues be fully addressed and a coordination rule for monetary policy explicitly be accepted. Without this, the EMS will remain an interesting but unsuccessful experiment and stage two of EMU a never-ending phase.

Comment

WOLFGANG RIEKE

Before discussing the Thygesen paper, I have two introductory remarks. First, I think that Peter Kenen's comments on this paper are very pertinent. This is not surprising, as Kenen has studied the EMS closely and is probably the number-one commentator on European monetary issues outside of Europe. Thus, in the course of my own discussion, I will likely reiterate some of his observations. Second, it is a formidable task to discuss in limited space the causes of crises within the EMS and what the Bundesbank and others are doing about it. I should also say that, coming from the Bundesbank, I offer these comments in my personal capacity.

My first point addresses the causes of the crises within the ERM during 1992–93. I think that Thygesen, referring to Eichengreen and Wyplosz, is correct in identifying two main causes: the absence of exchange rate realignments to correct for cumulative price and cost differentials among the members of the ERM and the foreign exchange markets' awareness of serious policy dilemmas in certain member countries. Thygesen is also right to argue that between 1992 and 1993 the latter became more important to the exchange markets than the former. But having listened to Kenen, I think that one should not make all that much of this shift in emphasis because the first crisis was triggered by the 1992 Danish referendum, which first raised the issue of policy credibility. The 1993 crisis was distinctive in that the French franc did not require a realignment, based on criteria used in the past. The emergence of policy dilemmas is

Wolfgang Rieke is Director, International Department, Deutsche Bundesbank.

often attributed to the shock of German unification and the debate about how or whether the ERM should be adjusted in response to the new circumstances, a topic on which Thygesen has much to say.

Exchange rate adjustments in the EMS had always corrected for divergence in prices and costs *ex post*. Revaluing the Deutsche mark in reaction to German unification in order to avert or ease some of its effects would have called for an *ex ante* agreement on the need for a shift in relative prices through a currency realignment. The EMS had no previous experience with decisions that anticipate rather than follow the accumulation of inflation differentials. As we know, such an agreement would have been difficult to achieve because governments wanted to safeguard the credibility of their stability policy by hanging on to the Deutsche mark as an anchor. An anticipatory revaluation of the D-mark would have also called into question the whole EMU, as that process had been premised on a smooth transition to the final stage without changing the central rates. Indeed, in my view the EMS as a fixed rate system with narrow bands derived its raison d'être in good part from its role as a precursor to EMU. We did not perceive this at the beginning of the EMU process, but that is what it became. Kenen's formulation on this subject is apt.

Why do I stress this point? Because the EMS was not likely to survive forever simply as a "zone of monetary stability in Europe," to quote the European Council resolution of Bremen in July 1978. From the very start it was obvious—at least to some, including myself—that a system of fixed-though-adjustable exchange rates with very narrow margins in Europe would at some point run into the same problems as the postwar Bretton Woods regime of fixed parities. This was not obvious at the beginning, but it was clear that financial markets would grow in size and sophistication and that they would integrate more closely and develop. Perhaps we had no notion of this happening so quickly, but I have always said that if the European Community did not arrive at a single currency within, say, 20 years, the system would explode in the meantime. Twenty years was a very rough estimate, and my observation was *not* a recommendation to go to a single currency, but this was the simple logic of a fixed rate system.

Like the old Bretton Woods regime, the EMS rests on several pillars. One pillar is the ability and willingness of participants to keep their own houses in order. The second pillar is their willingness to respect a minimum set of rules of behavior. The third pillar is the presence of a reliable anchor, and the fourth is a readiness to cooperate as necessary to deal with inconsistencies in monetary and other policies and to cooperate in the day-to-day management of exchange rates. A substantial measure of success has been achieved in monetary and exchange rate cooperation, despite the criticism that the whole crisis is due to a lack of cooperation. Some critics argue that if only the Bundesbank, for instance, had been more cooperative, then the narrow bands might have been saved. This is dubious. The EMS was bound to get into difficulties sooner or later simply because of the development of financial markets.

Why did the EMS not get into difficulties earlier? Because contrary to the original rules, which provided for the defense of exchange rates at the margin through potentially "unlimited" intervention, countries developed a preference for intramarginal intervention, which of course had the good effect of freeing the Bundesbank from concerns, regarding the effect of intervention on its monetary policy. Even without shocks as severe as German unification, the system could have gotten into trouble earlier if governments and central banks had relied exclusively on unlimited intervention at the margin and financed it through mutual credits. The Bundesbank flagged its concern about unlimited intervention at the margin by agreeing with the federal government that, in the event of a threat to the integrity of monetary policy in Germany by this intervention obligation or Bundesbank financing of intervention on the part of other central banks, the German government would ask for a realignment. This agreement, of course, was called upon in 1992, and it came into play again in 1993. The upshot of all this is that, as a guarantor of a zone of monetary stability in Europe, the old EMS probably had a limited life expectancy within which it would have been able to serve as a precursor of full monetary union if it had managed to avoid major crises in the meantime.

Now that we have an EMS with wider margins, wider even than some of us would have thought necessary, what are we to make of it? Will it still serve as a basis from which to move forward to EMU? Thygesen sees some redeeming features, some of which I find it easy to agree with. Importantly, for instance, the French franc was not a candidate for devaluation on any fundamental criteria, and the wide band, as Thygesen suggests, allows its central rate with respect to the D-mark to be maintained even in the face of adverse market sentiment. The same may apply to some of the other currencies. By contrast, Thygesen's interpretation of the new regime, according to which countries may move directly from their current rate to the future fixed rate when they feel ready to join the EMU, requires some qualification, which Thygesen himself supplies.

In any case, I, like others such as Kenen, do not see an early return to a narrow-margin system except on a selective basis. As you know, there is a bilateral agreement between Germany and the Netherlands on a narrow band. But such an agreement is possible only where governments are prepared to fully align themselves with the anchor country's monetary policy stance. I have already addressed the reasons for not going back to very narrow margins, citing in particular the role of financial markets. Measures to limit capital mobility, to which Thygesen refers, would be too high a price to pay for the return to the precrisis

EMS. In any event, capital controls would be ineffective when needed to defend the system, and most importantly they would be contrary to the single-market objective of the European Union and should be excluded for that reason as well. I am really surprised at the pronouncements, which have come from the top EU leadership, advocating a consideration of capital controls.

As a means to make exchange rate intervention more effective and thus make a fixed rate system more compatible with free capital movements and national control over monetary policy, the Bofinger proposal can only surprise those of us working at the Bundesbank. Bofinger's own stint working there must have failed to make much of an impression. The Bishop proposal seems hardly more appealing, and probably not only from the debtor central banks' viewpoint.

By contrast, collective monitoring of central banks' sterilization practices is likely to be part of the EMI's future tasks, although this monitoring will not be allowed to call into question national monetary policy responsibility in stage two. There should be no illusions, however, as to the scope for divorcing exchange market intervention and its effectiveness from decisions on domestic short-term interest rates. Even if the EMI were to be entrusted with certain operational tasks at some stage—which I have reason to doubt given its clearly defined and limited responsibilities—this would not be a device for countries "to have their cake and eat it too." Notions that Germany and its partners could all have had interest rate levels appropriate on domestic grounds while employing sterilization techniques that would have enabled the narrowband EMS to continue as before are just too farfetched to be taken seriously. Even in less agitated circumstances, reliance on sterilization gimmicks is questionable, and such techniques would probably quickly exhaust their usefulness. This is not to say, however, that sterilization techniques and their use in crisis circumstances are beyond critique—this topic deserves a seminar all by itself.

The really interesting scenario to examine, now that bands have been significantly widened, is that of a prolonged period under the new regime. The pessimistic scenario painted by Thygesen can, one hopes, be avoided, since it would seriously delay the resumption of the Maastricht process. Indeed, the temptation among the European countries to accept potential long-term costs, in terms of allowing inflation to accelerate again and failing to qualify for membership in the monetary union, in exchange for uncertain short-term gains, in terms of lower interest rates, appears to be small enough at the moment. The experience of countries (such as the United Kingdom) that appeared to be able to realize such short-term gains by lowering their official interest rates aggressively after having left the ERM may yet serve to discourage others if the long-term benefits fail to materialize.

The British experience might have the further benefit of reducing the weight frequently given to interest rates as an instrument of macro-economic stabilization, especially by politicians who find it difficult to do what is necessary in other areas such as fiscal policy. This experience could underscore the need for countries across Europe to come to grips with fiscal deficits and thereby permit EMU to proceed on schedule. The German Constitutional Court has put additional emphasis on the need to meet the entry criteria for stage three, and the German government and the Bundesbank will not want to ignore these criteria.

My own view is that any forward movement on EMU will be multi-speed, with a limited group of countries that fulfill the convergence criteria by the date set in the Maastricht Treaty or sometime thereafter proceeding first, followed by other countries when the time is ripe. The risk remains that, all good intentions and declarations notwithstanding, the process will be delayed beyond the timetable set out in the treaty. Any return to narrow bands would probably have to be very temporary if intensive currency speculation is to be avoided. The genie is out of the bottle, and I am afraid that it will not easily be put back in. Financial markets will stay on the alert and will jump at the slightest chance of finding the authorities unable to defend the parities.

Now that the Maastricht Treaty has been fully ratified and has entered into force, it is highly desirable that the conditions for progress toward monetary union be fulfilled as planned. Some believe that the effort should be given up altogether and countries be left to fend for themselves under a regime of floating currencies in Europe. I would consider this view to be a counsel of despair rather than wisdom. But I hasten to add that the 1993 crisis has not made the task of completing monetary union any easier. Furthermore, the task will be made even more difficult—perhaps even hopeless—if certain illusions are perpetuated. Particularly harmful is the illusion that declarations of intent on the part of the European Union, as well as the announcement of programs and guidelines, will suffice to create the necessary conditions for progress. Only if such illusions are thoroughly dispelled and concrete actions replace good intentions in each and every country will EMU become reality.

WIDENING THE EUROPEAN UNION

4

EFTA Countries

PER MAGNUS WIJKMAN

The wider Europe that has emerged since the Berlin Wall fell has placed western countries and international institutions, economic and political, in an unexpected and sometimes awkward situation. The changed security situation in Europe has relaxed the foreign policy constraints that previously prevented most countries within the European Free Trade Association (EFTA) from considering accession to the European Community. Now, four years later, five EFTA countries have applied for membership in its successor, the European Union. Since "returning to Europe," a number of Central and Eastern European countries have stated their intention also to apply. Where does this leave the European Union? And where does it leave EFTA? Viewing themselves in the light of a wider Europe, these organizations have had to reconsider their roles.

Has the end of the Cold War left EFTA without a raison d'être? The first section of this paper considers the life expectancy of EFTA as an organization now that a number of its members are negotiating to join the European Union. Thereafter, it considers why some Central and Eastern European countries might find membership in EFTA to be a feasible second-best solution if membership in the European Union appears unlikely in this decade. Finally, it considers the measures necessary for the European Union, EFTA, and the European Economic Area (EEA) to serve as building blocs in a Pan-European architecture. The paper concludes that EFTA indeed has a role to play in integrating the wider Europe.

Per M. Wijkman is Director for Economic Affairs in the EFTA Secretariat. The views expressed in this paper do not necessarily reflect those of EFTA states or of the EFTA Secretariat. He thanks Richard Baldwin and Helen Wallace for constructive comments and discussion.

The wider Europe consists of those societies that adhere to the principles of community enrichment through diversity and protection of diversity through community. These twin principles define pretty clearly the limits of the wider Europe today.

Will EFTA Survive Enlargement of the European Union?

Four members of EFTA are currently negotiating the terms of accession to the European Union: Austria, Finland, Norway, and Sweden.[1] If these negotiations are concluded as planned and confirmed in national referendums to be held in each of them, EFTA will lose more than half of its members within a couple of years. An EFTA consisting of Switzerland, Iceland, and Liechtenstein would *probably* not be a viable organization. An EEA consisting of the European Union, Iceland, and Liechtenstein would *certainly* not be a viable construction. A close observer in the Commission Services (Grubben 1992) writes:

> Can the EEA survive accession of EFTA States to the Community? . . . Although the total number of parties to the EEA Agreement will remain the same, the EFTA pillar will be weakened progressively. This may have consequences for the institutional system on the EFTA side and in particular for the surveillance tasks, e.g. in the area of competition. Moreover, the Community may find it increasingly inefficient and cumbersome to have to go through all the joint procedures with a decreasing number of EFTA States. A 'critical mass' of the EFTA pillar for the EEA Agreement to function properly has not been defined, but the question will arise at some stage along the expected line of developments.[2]

The prospect of imminent enlargement of the European Union has consequently led to an expectation that the EEA will disappear and that EFTA itself is doomed as an organization. These expectations lead policymakers to treat EFTA as an organization without a future.

Whether or not this is justified depends on how imminent enlargement is. This section argues that the uncertainty surrounding the out-

---

1. However, Switzerland has also applied for accession to the European Union. The Swiss electorate rejected the EEA in a referendum on 6 December 1992. Negotiations between Switzerland and the European Union on membership therefore await clarification of the situation. Liechtenstein participates as an observer in the EEA. It will participate fully as soon as it has clarified the implications of EEA participation for application of its customs union with Switzerland.

2. High officials in the EFTA countries concerned have suggested that it would be impossible to operate the heavy administrative machinery of the EEA for only a few countries.

come of major European integration issues justifies a safety net in case the negotiations or referendums fail and argues that EFTA provides such a net.

EFTA and the EEA as a Safety Net

The view of EFTA's demise as imminent is based on two assumptions, both of which are uncertain: that all applicant countries will actually become European Union members and that this will occur soon. Neither can be taken for granted.

Likelihood of Membership

In each applicant country, the result of negotiations will be submitted to a national referendum. Opinion polls indicate that in no applicant country would a referendum, if held today, yield a yes to membership. An expected upturn in the business cycle will improve the odds for a positive outcome when referendums are eventually held. But even if only one country were to reject membership, this would mean that more than half of the current EFTA countries would remain in EFTA, raising the odds for its continued existence.

Timing of Membership

The countries currently negotiating accession to the European Union aimed initially to conclude these negotiations in 1994 and become members at the beginning of 1995. The negotiations were slow in starting and fell behind this timetable. However, they gathered momentum after the entry into force of the Maastricht Treaty on 1 November 1993, and the objective is to conclude them by March 1994 so they can be considered by the European Parliament before its summer recess. It is inevitable that negotiations will go faster with some applicants than with others. This will require the European Union to decide whether to give up its current policy of "bunching" applicants and instead admit them one by one as negotiations are concluded. If it "bunches," the pace of negotiations with the last country will determine when the negotiations with all four are concluded. The negotiation results must then be ratified by parliaments in EU countries as well as in EFTA countries. The date for accession is therefore dependent not only on how long negotiations take and the outcome of the referendums in EFTA countries, but also on the speed of ratification procedures in EU member states. The uncertainties and delays that characterized the process leading up to the entry into force of the Maastricht Treaty and the EEA Agreement suggest that many factors could delay accession. The worst-case scenario may be more realistic than the best-case scenario. While it is reasonable to use early 1995 as a best-case scenario for accession to the European Union, it may not always be the best bet with the "bookies."

Conclusions on EFTA's Survival

The two related uncertainties of "if" and "when" make it wise to hedge one's bets on EFTA's demise. Risk-averse governments have an interest in maintaining EFTA as a going concern in case accession fails, even if it is only their second-best choice. Unlike the desperate gambler who is tempted to up the ante and go for broke, governments will want to diversify their policy-option portfolios. Double or nothing is not for them. They will avoid burning their bridges by making self-fulfilling prophecies about EFTA's demise. EFTA is thus likely to be around longer than many expected a year ago, and probably at least until the end of the 1990s. Thus, it still constitutes an option. The next section considers the differences in the main options that face the countries of Central and Eastern Europe: EFTA and the European Union.

Available Options: European Union, EFTA cum EEA

Is EFTA an interesting option for others? Normally, it is useful to have several options. Consider the alternatives. Historically, the crucial difference between the European Community and EFTA as organizations has been the degree to which the participating countries in each group have been willing to share sovereignty—that is, to give up autonomy over their own policies in exchange for some influence over partner countries' policies.

The six founding members of the European Community were prepared to share sovereignty and develop supranational forms of cooperation. They saw economic integration as a means of achieving an ever-closer union that would make war in Europe impossible. They accepted majority voting and strove to expand the scope of EC activities. By contrast, EFTA was at the outset strictly limited to economic cooperation, which has not evolved to the degree that economic integration within the European Community has.[3] Furthermore, economic integration is limited to industrial goods, with agricultural products excluded. EFTA countries have traditionally had a strong preference for autonomy in decision making—especially in relations with third countries. Hence, EFTA is not a customs union but a free trade area, as its name implies, in which each member

---

3. The only extension of the scope of EFTA's activities has been the extension of free trade to saltwater fish and other marine products in 1990, 20 years after the accession of Iceland, whose major export commodity is fish.

conducts its own external trade policy. In short, while the European Community saw economic integration as a means for achieving political union, the EFTA countries have pursued economic integration, as an end in itself, as far as is possible without political union.

As a result of the differing preferences of member states, the two organizations differ strikingly. EFTA is a typical intergovernmental organization, limited strictly to economic matters, in which each country has its own external commercial policy and in which decisions are made by consensus. The secretariat is small and provides services to the EFTA countries. In contrast, the European Union has an evolutionary character, extending cooperation to a variety of fields, some political. Its institutions possess important supranational powers. Decisions are taken by majority voting in an increasing number of fields. The European Commission has the right to propose legislation and strong powers of surveillance over member states' compliance with legislation. The European Court of Justice ensures enforcement of EU rules.

The EFTA countries have significantly extended the scope of their integration with EU states through the agreement on the European Economic Area (EEA). In force as of the beginning of 1994, the agreement is a compromise that precariously combines salient characteristics of both the EU and EFTA. It extends EU rules concerning industrial goods, services, capital movements, and people to the EFTA countries. But unlike the internal market, it maintains the autonomy of the contracting parties, in particular vis-à-vis third countries. As a result, the EEA does not include policies requiring common decision making and management institutions such as a common commercial policy including a customs union, a common agricultural policy, a common fisheries policy, a currency and monetary union, or regional and structural income transfers.

Because of these basic differences, the existence of the European Union and EFTA *cum* EEA provides European countries with a range of options. Together, these options represent a set of concentric circles leading to progressively deeper integration (figure 1). In theory, this set of circles allows a country to proceed from an institution providing primarily free trade in industrial goods (EFTA), via one embracing most of the four freedoms (EEA) to an economic, monetary, and political union (EC/EU). At the same time, these concentric circles lead from decision making by consensus to majority voting. This diversity allows countries in Central and Eastern Europe to choose the option that best suits their needs, subject to constraints imposed by feasibility. Before turning to these constraints, it is worth noting that neither option is ideal for them.

EU Membership Now: An Unattainable Best Option

For most EFTA governments, membership in the European Union is their first choice. This is true for the Central and Eastern Europeans as

Figure 1 Concentric circles of the European architecture

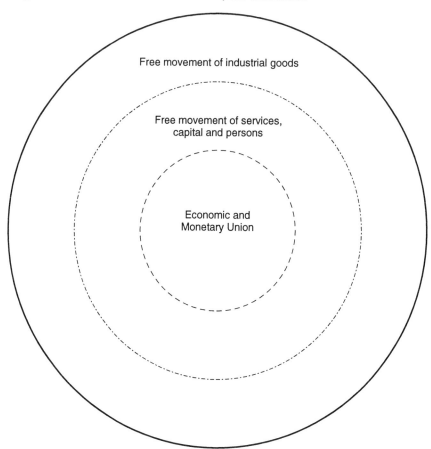

Free movement of industrial goods

Free movement of services,
capital and persons

Economic and
Monetary Union

The circles represent institutions of increasing degrees of integration and not geography. Nonetheless, they correspond largely to the concentric circles on a map
of Europe—with important exceptions. Thus, the geographically most central countries of Europe tend to lie in the innermost institutional circle, but Switzerland
does not and the European Union includes countries on the geographic periphery
of Europe (Greece, Portugal). The outermost circle, providing free trade in industrial goods, contains many countries that lie in the geographic center of Europe
(Slovenia, Czech Republic).

well. For them, the European Union appears as the light at the end of
the tunnel in their transition to market economies. The Europe agreements that were concluded first with Poland, Hungary, the Czech Republic, and Slovakia, and later with Bulgaria and Romania, record each
country's ambition to become a member state of the European Union.
The preamble of these agreements notes that the "final objective of [the
country] is to become a member of the Community, and this association,
in view of the parties, will help to achieve this objective."

While the European Community at the Copenhagen Summit in 1993 did not commit itself to a timetable, it did endorse the principle of accession and the general criteria.[4] Accession is thus in one sense only a question of time. The Union has been hesitant to open similar negotiations with additional countries because of the implied commitment to membership.[5]

However, EU membership for the countries of Central and Eastern Europe is not likely soon. This is in part because major changes in EU internal policies will be necessary to accommodate these countries as members.[6] The Common Agricultural Policy would generate unsustainable agricultural surpluses if such countries as Poland and Hungary became members, making revision inevitable. The current rules of the structural and regional funds would generate large income transfers to the East, calling for increased revenues from the current members and/or reduced transfers to current beneficiaries. The significant gap in wages between Eastern and Western countries might give rise to migration of labor on a scale that strains the willingness of governments to countenance the free movement of people. Major changes are inevitable. It is unrealistic to expect the European Union to make them at a time when it is engaged in enlargement, institutional reform, implementation of economic and monetary union, and the evolution of common foreign, security, and defense policies. Change will require time. Thus, membership for these countries is not feasible in this century and may take many years into the next decade.[7] This premise is crucial for what follows.

EFTA Membership Now: An Attainable Second-Best

Given that EU membership for countries in Central and Eastern Europe appears to be far off in time, EFTA could be an attractive transitional

---

4. These criteria for the prospective applicants include the capacity to assume the *acquis communautaire*; the stability of institutions guaranteeing democracy, the rule of law, human rights, and respect for minorities; the existence of a functioning market economy; the endorsement of the objectives of political, economic, and monetary union, and the capacity to cope with competitive pressure and market forces within the Union. The Union's capacity to absorb new members while maintaining the momentum of European integration is also mentioned.

5. The European Union started exploratory talks with Slovenia on a Europe agreement in December 1993; negotiations are expected to start in the first half of 1994.

6. This view is presented, for example, in Baldwin et al. (1992).

7. These problems would be ameliorated by admitting only one Central or Eastern European country into the European Union. There are strong barriers against admitting these countries selectively, however. Politically, once one country is let into the Union, it would be impossible to draw the line. Hence, it is most likely that none will be let in until several of them are admitted.

arrangement—the traditional role of EFTA as a waiting room and training school.[8] While being in a waiting room provides advantages, for some it risks prolonging the wait.[9] These countries must therefore weigh the advantages of being in EFTA now against the disadvantages of prolonging the wait to enter the European Union. Those that face a long wait because they are at the end of the queue may find that the transitional advantages of EFTA membership predominate. For some countries, EFTA membership might even shorten the wait because EFTA, as a training school in economic integration, prepares them for membership in the European Union. Those countries that have made slow progress in the transition to a market economy or started late may find EFTA membership especially useful.

On the other hand, countries such as Hungary or Poland that believe they have progressed rapidly in the transition to a market economy and are already at the head of the queue to enter the European Union may find that a sojourn in EFTA delays their entry.

This suggests that the countries most likely to find EFTA membership attractive are Albania, the Baltic states, Bulgaria, Romania, and Slovenia. Albania and Slovenia are particularly likely to find EFTA accession attractive since they have no free trade agreements with EFTA countries and would therefore have a strong economic interest in EFTA membership. This may also be true of the Baltic states, even though they have bilateral free trade agreements with most EFTA countries. They must ask themselves how secure these bilateral agreements are, given that the applicant EFTA countries will adopt EU external commercial policy once they become members. At present, the European Union does not provide for free trade with the Baltic states.[10] The Baltic states might therefore wish to improve the prospects of maintaining the existing free trade arrangements with most EFTA countries. EFTA membership would be one way to do this.

Will EFTA accept new applicants? The answer is not self-evident. EFTA decisions require unanimity, and views among current EFTA members are likely to be split. On the one hand, EFTA applicants are currently fully occupied with their membership negotiations with the European

---

8. The role of EFTA as a complement to and preparation for EU membership is indicated already in the preamble to the Stockholm Convention:

> . . . determined to facilitate the early establishment of a multilateral association for the removal of trade barriers and the promotion of closer economic cooperation between the Members of the Organisation for European Economic Co-operation in the European Economic Community.

9. The pros and cons of EFTA membership are analyzed in Baldwin (1992).

10. The European union started exploratory talks on free trade agreements with the Baltic states at the end of 1993 and is considering a mandate for formal negotiations.

Union. They can ill afford to be distracted from this major objective by EFTA enlargement. They no doubt wish to avoid enlargement on two fronts simultaneously. On the other hand, the EFTA nonapplicant states are likely to be positive toward EFTA enlargement because it increases its critical mass. The same is true of risk-averse EFTA applicants. There is thus likely to be a majority for EFTA enlargement at the moment, but no unanimity.

This situation is likely to change. The closer the EFTA applicants come to EU membership, the more they will tend to think like EU members. This means that they might increasingly prefer having the Central and Eastern European countries in EFTA than in the European Union. The distractions of future EU enlargement will outweigh the distractions of enlarging EFTA now. Thus, an EFTA consensus on EFTA enlargement is likely to emerge in 1994.

Which candidates for EFTA membership are the most likely to be accepted? The following characteristics appear important. Successful candidates should be small, highly industrial, and with relatively high per capita income levels.[11] They should be adjacent to an existing EFTA member and have at least one strong advocate within EFTA, ideally in the EFTA chair when they submit their application.

These considerations would appear to rule out Albania on many counts. Among other strong candidates for EFTA accession, Latvia and Lithuania are not adjacent to EFTA countries, although some might argue that water connects rather than separates. Slovakia is adjacent to Austria for a short stretch but has lower per capita income than other candidates. This leaves Estonia and Slovenia as the most acceptable candidates.

Slovenia appears to be the prime candidate on several counts. It is small, highly industrial and has the highest per capita income in the East (Salay 1992). It is adjacent to Austria, with which it has many close and long ties. It has a strong economic interest in membership since it has no free trade agreements with any EFTA country.[12] It has a strong political interest in membership, since this would anchor it more securely in the center of Europe, to which it historically has belonged as part of Charlemagne's empire and the Holy Roman Empire.

Estonia is also a strong candidate for EFTA accession on similar grounds, but the economic arguments for membership are weaker than for Slovenia since Estonia already has free trade agreements with most

---

11. This last is a political rather than an economic requirement. Gains from trade arise from trade between countries with widely different per capita income levels. However, the formation of free trade areas is based on concepts of reciprocity and balance, which may be difficult to realize if per capita income levels differ too much.

12. The EFTA countries were to start exploratory talks on a free trade agreement with Slovenia in January 1994.

EFTA countries. The political argument for institutional anchoring in the West, how-ever, should be at least as great as for Slovenia, if not greater, due to the chaotic conditions in Estonia's eastern neighbor. Since the early 13th century, Estonia has had close economic and cultural contacts with West European nations.

Summary of Options

Central and East European countries are looking for an organization that provides strong political anchorage and gradual economic integration. Neither EFTA nor the European Union is an ideal solution for them. The looser economic integration represented by EFTA, when combined with the option of the EEA, is an attractive economic proposition that is available for much of Central and Eastern Europe now but provides insufficient political anchorage. The European Union provides political anchorage, but precisely because of its intensive degree of economic integration, is not now a feasible option. The appropriate institutional framework must combine features of both EFTA and the European Union. This would reconcile the Union's legitimate concerns about pursuing its own consolidation and deepening with Central and Eastern Europe's need for closer integration and political anchoring with the countries of Western Europe. The next section considers this possibility.

Building Blocs of the Pan-European Architecture

An organizational framework characterized by variable geometry is necessary to accommodate the diversity represented by the East and West of Europe. If this variability is not provided within the European Union, it must be provided outside the Union but with its active participation. There are today no indications that the Union's scope for multispeed integration and variable geometry is anywhere large enough to accommodate the diversity contained within the wider Europe. Rather than address the problem, the tendency in some quarters is to hope that it will disappear as the passage of time reduces economic disparities. Aware of the high political risks of such a policy of benign neglect, the European Commission has advocated EU creation of an institutional framework that includes the countries of Central and Eastern Europe.

Creating a Variable Geometry

Linking existing institutions such as EFTA, the EEA, and the European Union together and providing the countries in Central and Eastern Europe with an entry point would create a variable geometry capable of accommodating diversity. Building on existing institutions would be an expeditious—if not elegant—solution. Time is of the essence, and such a solution in a timely fashion is better than an elegant solution that is tardy. This section therefore considers what principles are essential to join the existing building blocs into a framework that merits being called a European architecture rather than an organizational labyrinth.

A first principle is that the framework should be Pan-European in scope, including all market economies in the wider Europe that are pluralistic democracies observing human rights. The concept of a Pan-European free trade area for goods was endorsed by the Community at the Copenhagen Summit in June 1993 and is supported by the EFTA countries. It would reflect present political realities and emerging economic realities. The political reality is that Europe is again whole and free. The economic reality is that the rapidly growing trade flows between the former planned economies in the East of Europe and the market economies in the West are tying these natural trading partners closer together. Three years after the fall of the Berlin Wall, Bulgaria, Czechoslovakia, Hungary, Poland, and Romania already conduct over half of their total trade with the countries of the European Union and EFTA.[13]

A second principle is that there should be possibilities to progress gradually to more intensive forms of integration over time. There should be a clear progression from one institution to another, and this progression should be open to any European country that fulfills specified requirements. In September 1993, President of the European Commission Jacques Delors proposed that the EEA be open also for countries in Central and Eastern Europe:

> On a practical note, I propose to draw up a precise plan of action and procedures for stabilizing the situation in Central and Eastern Europe, responding to their security needs and linking them stage by stage to the Community—beginning with association, then accession to the European Economic Area, and finally Community membership, the ultimate goal.[14]

---

13. The importance of these countries for the EU and EFTA countries is much smaller due primarily to their smaller economic mass. However, Richard Baldwin (1993) predicts that their importance will have increased dramatically once the transition to a market economy has been completed and per capita income levels have caught up to the average level in Western Europe. Using a gravity model of trade, he estimates that trade flows between East and West Europe will grow at two-digit levels during the next one to two decades. Trade growth will be particularly rapid for most EFTA countries due to their geographical location. One-quarter of the growth of EFTA exports to Europe will consist of exports to countries in Central and Eastern Europe.

14. This proposal, made in a speech at the International Institute of Strategic Studies in London on 10 September 1993, was the only section of the speech to be put in bold type in the European Commission's press release.

Since accession to the EEA presupposes membership in EFTA (or in the European Union), Delors was in fact proposing that EFTA serve these countries as their entry point into the European architecture. The interlinking of these institutions, constituting different levels of integration, would create interconnected concentric circles in Europe. Countries encompassed by the larger outer circle would participate in a free trade area for industrial goods. Countries encompassed by the second largest circle would in addition participate in the free movement of services, capital, and people. Finally, the European Union would constitute the inner circle, characterized by limited internal scope for multispeed integration and variable geometry.

A third principle is that widening and deepening in accordance with the principles laid out above should be achieved in a transparent and efficient manner in order to minimize transaction costs for economic operators and management costs for governments. This means minimizing the number of agreements necessary to achieve eventually free movement of goods, services, capital, and people among the countries of Europe. The number of trade agreements that are needed is determined both by the number of countries and the number of markets (goods, services, capital, etc.) to be integrated in each particular instance. Widening and deepening at differential rates on an ad hoc basis is likely to result in an organizational labyrinth.

Simplifying the Current Hub-and-Spoke Pattern

The current trade policy framework in Europe hardly reflects these principles and as a result is becoming increasingly labyrinthine, as figure 2 illustrates. Basically, it is a hub-and-spoke structure, schematically portrayed in figure 3. Such a structure has at least three major drawbacks for countries that are spokes. First, it is costly for economic operators to work under the plethora of bilateral trade agreements, so they tend to concentrate trade and investment flows within the hubs at the expense of the spokes. This tendency is further encouraged by rules of origin, which tend to limit cumulation of origin to the parties to each bilateral trade agreement. Thus, a product using components from several spokes and being exported ultimately to a country in the hub, will tend to be produced in the hub rather than in one of the spokes. Secondly, each spoke country discriminates against other spoke countries' products in favor of products from the hub. Thirdly, each spoke country is marginalized politically, and its bargaining position vis-à-vis the countries in the hub is relatively weak.

In a hub-and-spoke structure it is hardly surprising that countries strive to become members of the largest hub, the European Union. However, for reasons mentioned previously, this is likely to take decades. Until then, it

Figure 2 Central and Eastern Europe: pattern of free trade agreements

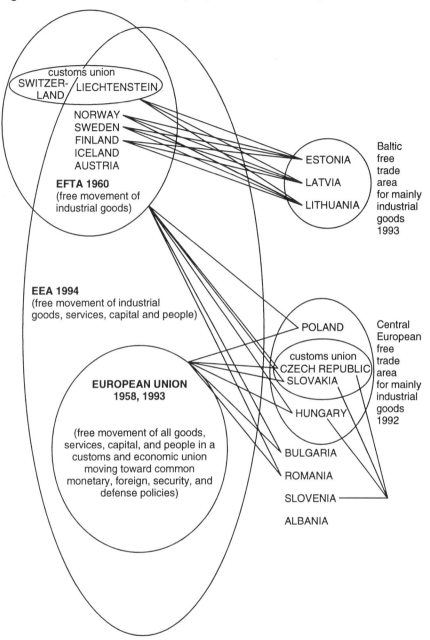

Connecting straight lines indicate the existence of initialed, signed, ratified, or applied free trade agreements between a country, or group of countries, and countries in Central and Eastern Europe.

Figure 3 Hub-and-spoke pattern of free trade agreements for industrial goods

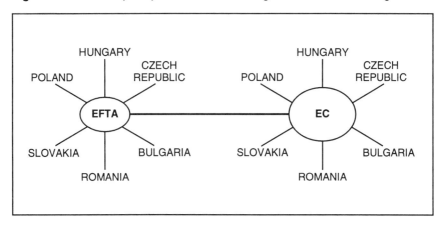

The free trade agreements of 1972 between each EFTA country and the Community are bilateral agreements. Some improvements were introduced in 1988 whereby components originating in any EFTA country and in the EC countries (multilateral cumulation) were entitled to tariff-free trade. The formally bilateral FTAs will be largely superseded by the EEA Agreement, which will allow components originating in any EFTA country to qualify for tariff-free trade when the final product is traded within the EEA even if substantial transformation has not taken place in each individual EFTA country or in the Community (full cumulation). Similar benefits are not enjoyed by production facilities located in the spokes.

is necessary to find interim arrangements to simplify the increasingly complex hub and spoke pattern that is emerging. One way to do this is to encourage the spokes to join other hubs and to connect the hubs, thereby reducing the number of spokes relative to the number of hubs.

Connecting the Spokes

In a hub-and-spoke structure, the spokes are not connected with each other by free trade agreements. Each spoke thus discriminates against other spokes in favor of countries in the hub. The resulting trade diversion may be considerable. The analysis in Baldwin (1993) predicts that the countries in Central and Eastern Europe will conduct about one-third of their European trade with each other after their transition to a market economy and a feasible economic catchup to Western Europe. To allow these natural trade flows to develop, free trade among these countries needs to be established *pari passu* with their integration with the West. Some spokes are currently doing this by setting up bilateral free trade agreements between them, creating a rim connecting the spokes.[15]

---

15. Slovenia has initialed or signed free trade agreements with three other countries in Central and Eastern Europe. Other countries have made similar advances but without success.

However, this is an inefficient way to connect all the spokes. For instance, 66 bilateral agreements would be necessary to connect 12 countries. Since the agreements are unlikely to be identical, such a complex system generates high information costs and is extremely costly for economic agents—both traders and investors.

Creating New Hubs

A more efficient way to achieve free trade would be for a number of spokes to join together and form new hubs or join existing ones. This is an efficient way to establish free trade among the countries in the hub because it contributes to uniformity: the participating countries sign a single, multilateral agreement. Thus, the four Central European countries created the Central European Free Trade Area (CEFTA) in 1992 and the Baltic states agreed on a Baltic Free Trade Area in industrial goods in 1993. However, these mini-hubs do not appear to be open to new members, having been created primarily at the encouragement of the then— European Community in order to allow for improved cumulation of origin. In fact, the countries of Central and Eastern Europe do not appear attracted to the idea of establishing free trade among themselves by expanding a hub such as CEFTA. A hub consisting only of countries of Central and Eastern Europe smacks to them of CMEA *redivivus*. For these countries, the key aim is to gain access to markets in Western Europe, not to establish free trade with other countries in Eastern Europe.

Connecting the Hubs

Transparency and uniformity are fostered if free trade between countries in two hubs is established by a single agreement between the hubs. This requires that the countries in *each* hub conduct a common commercial policy—that is, form a customs union rather than a free trade area. This is the case only for the European Union. Hence, its 12 members have the same trade agreement with any country in one of the other groups. In principle, the European Union has as many trade agreements as there are countries in EFTA or CEFTA, since the latter maintain autonomy with regard to third-country relations. However, the Community has aimed to have uniform agreements with countries in each particular group. For instance, the EC's free trade agreements with EFTA countries of 1972 are formally bilateral but are virtually identical. These bilateral agreements were replaced by the multilateral EEA agreement in 1994.

Also, the EFTA countries have increasingly been conducting a de facto common commercial policy toward other countries in Europe. The EFTA countries together have negotiated a free trade agreement for industrial goods with each of six countries in Central and Eastern Europe. These six agreements are largely identical. EFTA countries' de facto common policy vis-à-vis countries in Central and Eastern Europe is furthermore closely coordinated with EU policy. However, a number of differences remain. Trade in agricultural products has been negotiated bilaterally by each EFTA country, and not jointly as in the European Union. The Europe agreements extend beyond industrial goods further than the corresponding EFTA agreements. Developments point toward a de facto common commercial policy regarding industrial goods by the European Union and EFTA countries vis-à-vis the rest of Europe. This suggests and facilitates taking the next step toward a multilateral agreement of the type represented by the EEA.

EFTA as a Possible Hub

It is possible that EFTA will fade away rapidly, leaving the European Union as the sole hub in Europe. It is possible that this hub will attach other European countries to it through bilateral agreements, as now, or that it will create a new institution for Pan-European trade, an "Association of Association Agreements" in Richard Baldwin's felicitous phrase. But it is equally possible that EFTA survives EU enlargement and expands as a hub because it provides a tried and tested, graduated approach to European integration. Countries that choose EFTA will do so because they realize that membership in the European Union, their first choice, will take decades. Therefore, they need an interim solution providing limited integration to start with and the possibility of conducting an autonomous commercial policy. Although CEFTA cannot, membership in EFTA provides this political anchoring in a Western institution with a proven track record. True, it does not provide a security umbrella, but what institution is offering that today? True, it does not include free trade in agricultural goods, but precisely because the European Union does, agricultural producers in Eastern Europe are precluded from EU membership! True, EFTA does not provide income transfers on as big a scale as does the European Union, but it can do so on a small scale: witness the Industrial Development Fund for Portugal and the similar one EFTA countries set up for Yugoslavia just before that country disintegrated.

Above all, EFTA constitutes the outer circle of the European architecture and provides the entry point into the next circle: the EEA. The EEA provides an easy way to multilateralize the current flowering of bilateral trade agreements, perhaps when the transition periods in these agreements expire in 2002. It should also prove possible to apply the provisions of the EEA concerning services, capital, and people flexibly by allowing significant transition periods for those freedoms that prove problematic.

At the EFTA ministerial meeting in December 1993 in Vienna, Austrian Minister of Economy Wolfgang Schüssel, who then held the EFTA chair, noted two conditions for EFTA enlargement: applicant countries must take the initiative, and the European Union must agree. The latter is natural because a number of common issues are involved, in particular the development of a de facto common commercial policy toward European countries and the continued provision of technical and financial assistance efficiently on a sufficient scale.

Conclusion

The end of the Cold War has overnight created a wider Europe. In this wider Europe, EFTA's traditional role as a waiting room and training school in European integration is needed more than ever. Changing circumstances have allowed some EFTA members to progress to more intensive forms of integration, but others still find EFTA their first choice, and countries in the wider Europe find EFTA a feasible second-best. This indicates that EFTA retains its raison d'être.

Now that the Maastricht Treaty and the EEA agreement have entered into force and the accession negotiations will soon be completed, the next item on the political agenda is how to integrate the countries of Central and Eastern Europe into the wider Europe. At one extreme, European statesmen let the current hub-and-spoke pattern develop on an ad hoc basis; at the other, they create from scratch a Pan-European free trade area on a multilateral basis. In between stands the option to link the existing institutions together so they form a European architecture. This intermediate approach will require decisive action by political leaders in the European Union and in the countries of EFTA and Central and Eastern Europe. Time is of the essence, and as far as the EFTA option is concerned, the window of opportunity is rapidly closing. This is no time for indecision. It may be useful to recall the admonition in Goethe's *Faust*:

> Lose this day loitering—'twill be the same story
> Tomorrow—and the next more dilatory:
> Then indecision brings its own delays,
> And days are lost lamenting o'er lost days.
> Are you in earnest? Seize this very minute—
> What you can do, or dream you can, begin it.
> Courage has genius, power and magic in it.
> Only engage, and then the mind grows heated—
> Begin it, and the work will be completed.

References

Baldwin, Richard. 1992. *An Eastern Enlargement of EFTA: Why the East Europeans should join and the EFTAns should want them.* CEPR Occasional Paper No. 10. London: Centre for Economic Policy Research (November).

Baldwin, Richard. 1993. *The Potential for Trade Between the Countries of EFTA and Central and Eastern Europe*. EFTA Occasional Paper No. 44. Geneva: EFTA (June).

Baldwin, Richard, et al. 1992. *Is Bigger Better? The Economics of EC Enlargement*. CEPR Special Report No. 3. London: Center for Economic Policy Research.

Commission of the European Communities. 1992a. *Europe and the Challenge of Enlargement*. Report to the European Council, Lisbon (June).

Commission of the European Communities. 1992b. *Towards a Closer Association with the Countries of Central and Eastern Europe*. Report to the European Council, Edinburgh (December).

Commission of the European Communities. 1993. *Towards a Closer Association with the Countries of Central and Eastern Europe*. Communication to the Council in view of the meeting of the European Council, Copenhagen (June).

European Free Trade Association (EFTA). 1993. *Patterns of Production and Trade in the New Europe*. Geneva: European Free Trade Association.

Grubben, Marian. 1992. "The EEA and EFTA: Status and Perspectives." Presentation at conference on The European Economic Era—The EFTA States after 1992, London, 4 June.

Kostrzewa, Wojciech, and Holger Schmiedling. 1989. *The EFTA option for Eastern Europe: Towards an Economic Reunification of the Divided Continent*. Kieler Arbeitspapier 397. Kiel (October).

Michalski, Anna, and Helen Wallace. 1992. *The Challenge of Enlargement*. RIAA Special Papers 1. London: Royal Institute of International Affairs.

Norberg, Sven, et al. 1993. *EEA Law; The European Economic Area: A Commentary on the EEA Agreement*. Stockholm: Fritzes.

Rollo, Jim, and Alasdair Smith. 1993. "The Political Economy of Eastern European Trade with the European Community: Why so Sensitive?" *Economic Policy* 16 (April).

Salay, Jurgen. 1992. *An Economic Survey of Slovenia and Croatia*. EFTA Occasional Paper No. 42. Geneva: EFTA (December).

Wijkman, Per Magnus. 1993. "The Existing Bloc Expanded? The European Community, EFTA, and Eastern Europe." In C. Fred Bergsten and Marcus Noland, *Pacific Dynamism and the International Economic System*. Washington: Institute for International Economics.

Comment

PENTTI VARTIA

Per Wijkman's diagram of a European architecture of concentric circles is pedagogically very useful. I agree with him that there is much room for coordination of the European free trade agreements particularly and of trade policies generally. As previous chapters have illustrated, many Central and Eastern European countries consider the European Union to be the best alternative at the moment, but it may be a long time before they can join. In the meantime, we should work with existing institutions to coordinate European policies.

The benefits from trade and other forms of integration, of course, do not depend upon the names of organizations that establish the functioning of the markets but how well they accomplish this task. There are many organizations, and some rivalry among organizations may even be beneficial. Also, the IMF, World Bank, OECD, GATT, and CEFTA will have their roles in European integration.

Wijkman points out that EFTA has proved it can coordinate free trade agreements well. Of course, a major reason for EFTA's success is that coordinating free trade of industrial goods is easier than coordinating agricultural policies or labor mobility.

Yet it is easy to see how Wijkman's enlarged EFTA could develop into a very heterogeneous group of countries with conflicting goals. Some present members might feel a little awkward if left alone with the new members. EFTA should also offer something more than GATT and the Europe agreements.

Pentti Vartia is Managing Director of the Research Institute of the Finnish Economy (ETLA) in Helsinki.

Wijkman points out that the countries of Central and Eastern Europe are more important for many EFTA countries than they are for EU members on average. This will be true even if EFTA countries join the Union. From their perspective, the idea that Central and Eastern European countries should join EFTA when they themselves join the European Union is thus sound. This way, the EU entrants could have better trade relations with new EFTA entrants than they would have otherwise. A problem related to the proposal is that some EFTA countries' entrance to the Union is uncertain. Thus governments have to consider the possibility that they will stay in EFTA after the Central and Eastern European countries have joined. There are substantial differences between these countries and current EFTA members. Some of the countries of Central and Eastern Europe are large; the population in the five largest of these countries is around 100 million, while the population in EFTA is 30 million. Some of Central and Eastern Europe is poor: EFTA's GNP per capita is five to three times higher. The countries have different industrial structures, with Central and Eastern Europe more dependent on agriculture.

A related question is, if the current EFTA members join the European Union, will the EU-EFTA relationship be the same? Some EU countries may, for example, want to use more protective measures against the "new" EFTA. Because of these and many other uncertainties, decisions related to EFTA's future may have to wait until we know what happens to the EU membership applications of Austria, Finland, Norway, and Sweden.

In the following section I discuss some complementary ideas regarding the linkage between economic and political developments, labor mobility, and decision making in the enlarged European Union.

Economics and Politics

Developments in past years have once again shown how important international politics is for small European countries. The collapse of the Soviet empire did not radically change the political and economic situation only in Eastern Europe. It also radically altered the political constraints of the small EFTA countries that in Cold War terminology were typically called neutral. We should keep the lessons of history in mind: international politics will be equally important in the future. When discussing the potential membership of EFTA, we should also have some view on future political developments in Russia. Russia is a big and very heterogeneous country that extends to the Pacific Ocean. The literature on the optimal currency area suggests that it is too big for a monetary union. How can a country of this size participate in European integration?

Political developments are in many ways directly related to present economic decisions. Direct investments and the choice of production locations depends on political expectations. Let us think, for example, of foreign direct investment in Baltic countries. This argument is also important for the small EFTA countries with international firms. The biggest Finnish firms typically have close to 50 percent of their capacity abroad, and decisions on where to invest are very much dependent on expectations of the future structure of Europe. One reason for investment moves outside Sweden's and Finland's borders in the 1980s was the belief that these countries would stay outside the European Community.[1] Investments are important for the recovery in Europe, and it is a pity that at present many uncertainties postpone necessary investment projects.

Labor Mobility

Among the four freedoms—goods, services, capital, people—the free movement of labor offers the greatest problems. In some opinion polls, a large share of the population in Eastern European countries has expressed a willingness to migrate. In a recent opinion poll, 15 percent of the inhabitants in St. Petersburg, for example, expressed their desire to move to the West (EVA 1993). Perhaps we should draw an extra circle in Wijkman's diagram to differentiate the phases where labor movements become free.

As for the European Union, it seems that while obstacles to movement of EU citizens will be abolished, the governments want to retain some power to determine the treatment of non-EU nationals. However, a common migration policy must be in place for the internal labor market to function properly.

Labor movements within the present European Union are an easy issue for the EFTA entrants to the Union. According to some Nordic studies, joining the Union would not have large effects on migration flows between the EFTA entrants and the EU-12. There may be some movement of low-paid workers toward the Nordic countries, and part of their educated labor force may flee Scandinavian high taxes.

Potential labor flows from the Central and Eastern European countries pose a major question for many EFTA countries. Big differences in standards of living have developed between European countries in recent decades. Even if the Union's immigration restrictions are tightened, emigration from Eastern Europe is on the increase, and this will be an important issue for the Nordic countries, which since the 1950s have

---

1. For discussion of direct investments in Nordic countries see, for example, ETLA et al. (1990) and Alho and Widgrén (1993).

had a common labor market, and Austria. If Finland becomes an EU member, its long border with Russia also becomes the European Union's border with Russia. Finland is closer than others, for example, to the densely populated St. Petersburg region. Labor mobility considerations rule out full membership in the EEA or European Union for many Eastern European countries for years to come.

Decision Making

Decision making is an important aspect related to Wijkman's model of concentric circles and progression from one institutional level to the next. When the European Union is widened, this question will undoubtedly be put on the table. Of course, the enlargement itself brings many problems related to the division of decision-making power between the present members and the entrants (Widgrén 1991 and 1994). Creating decision-making institutions that correspond to the different levels of circles is a major challenge for future research. One reason certain EEA members want to become EU members is so they can participate in decision making. It is likely that this will hold true in the future as well. Thus the EEA may not be a very stable solution.

References

Alho, Kari, and Mika Widgrén. 1991. *Voting Power in the EC and the Consequences of Two Different Enlargements*. Helsinki: ETLA (DP 377).

Alho, Kari, and Mika Widgrén. 1993. *The Danish EC Experience: A Finnish Point of View.* Helsinki: ETLA (B 85).

Alho, Kari, and Mika Widgrén. 1994. "Voting Power in the Council of Ministers before and after the Enlargement of the EC." In Baldwin, Haaparanta, and Kiander, *Extending European Regionalism.*

Centre for Finnish Business and Policy Studies (EVA). 1993. *Business in St. Petersburg–An Economic and Cultural Review.* Helsinki: EVA.

Research Institute of the Finnish Economy (ETLA). 1990. *Integration in the Nordic Perspective.* Helsinki: ETLA.

Comment

THOMAS LACHS

I am in broad agreement with Per Wijkman and accept the general thrust of his paper. I am, however, less optimistic than he is about the negotiations between the European Union and EFTA. Given the likely progress of these negotiations, I would say that a job with EFTA is secure employment.

With the development of the single market and the end of the division of Europe, the EFTA countries became strongly interested in closer links to the European Community. The end of the Cold War removed political obstacles to EC membership, for the neutral countries in particular. The Community did not respond enthusiastically. I suspect that the original intention of the proposal for the European Economic Area (EEA) was not to create for the EFTA countries a stepping stone into the Community but rather to avoid admitting EFTA countries as members. In the end most of us in the EFTA countries concluded that the EEA would be a step forward.

For these reasons, we in EFTA are all the more disappointed—even shocked—that the countries of the European Union are obviously so little interested in the EEA. I may remind you that they are already taking more than a year to ratify a not very complicated treaty that they all say they love.

The European Union does not look very enticing from the outside at the moment, but the Central and East European countries want to join it anyway. They are all in favor of European unification, just as the East

Thomas Lachs is Executive Director of the Austrian National Bank.

Germans were in favor of German unification. I hope very much that Central and Eastern Europe will not experience the same disappointments that Germany has.

First of all, Central and East European countries are underestimating the difficulty of getting into the European Union. The EFTA countries are learning this through painful experience.

Secondly, Central and Eastern Europe have overestimated Western Europe's interest in them. By now they should have realized that this interest is mainly rhetorical and will not be backed up by any real deeds.

The recession is making entry into the European Union more difficult. The former Soviet Union is probably going to become the much more pressing problem for Western Europe. The previous panel discussed emergency measures that would have to be taken for Central and Eastern Europe. They probably will in fact have to be taken, but for the former Soviet Union rather than for Central and Eastern Europe.

As Per Wijkman has already pointed out, the European Union is very worried about Central and Eastern Europe, especially about migration of labor, about integrating these countries into the Common Agricultural Policy (which all of us know is its pet subject), and about the implications for structural and regional funds. Finally, and this is often overlooked, the European Union is concerned that enlargement will hamper its decision making unless accompanied by substantial institutional reform.

So I think that Central and Eastern European countries are going to have to wait a long time before they can really join the European Union. In this context, the EFTA would be a good waiting room because this waiting period is going to be much longer than most Central and Eastern Europeans now acknowledge.

Returning to the situation of the EFTA countries themselves, their negotiations with the European Union are already behind schedule, and the difficult problems have not even been really tackled. Take Austria as an example. There are three main problems: namely, agriculture, transit traffic, and second homes. What we have heard there mainly has been "no." As of October 1992, genuine negotiations had not actually begun.

What worries me most is that the EC negotiators think that their job is to win the negotiations, and they are trying hard to do this. This may be a human way of carrying out negotiations: you want your side to win. But if the EC negotiators do win, I think they can rest assured that the EFTA governments will lose their referendums.

And this brings me to the subject of referendums. Why should anybody vote for joining the European Union in the first place? It does not look that good from the outside. It has a huge recession with plenty of unemployment, and as we have just heard, the only way to get rid of this unemployment is to lower wages and social standards. We have seen that the people in the European Union are not all that happy—just look at the referendums in Denmark and France. There are all the troubles in the European Monetary System that we have talked about. Finally, there is the seriously deficient role that the Community has been playing vis-à-vis the former Yugoslavia.

Once the negotiations over accession to the European Union are completed, the governments of the EFTA applicants will submit their agreements to national referendums. Coming after the Maastricht Treaty has entered into force, these enlargement referendums will be unprecedented and extraordinarily difficult. The public opinion polls today, and Per Wijkman has talked about them, suggest that the chances of EU approval are weak in all but Finland. I remind you that in the referendums that have been carried out, both on joining the European Community and on Maastricht, in the runup to the referendum the side in favor lost 5 to 10 percentage points between the beginning of the campaign and the actual vote. If Austria loses that much, EU approval appears very much in doubt. I am reminded of an old children's rhyme, which, slightly modified, goes like this:

> Five little EFTA countries knocked on the EEA's door,
> In one the population said no, and then there were four.
>
> Four little EFTA countries wanted to join the EC,
> One couldn't negotiate a treaty, and then there were three.
>
> Three little EFTA countries asked their parliaments what to do,
> One parliament didn't like the idea, and then there were two.
>
> Two little EFTA countries thought a referendum would be fun,
> One could not get a majority, and then there was one.
>
> One little EFTA country thought everything had been done,
> But EU members didn't ratify, and then there were none.

I am not really as pessimistic as my nursery rhyme suggests. But I am afraid that the most likely scenario is that the negotiations between the European Union and EFTA will drag on well into 1995, that the referendums and the ratification process, wherever the referendums were successful, will take at least another year, extending the process into 1996 and 1997. In all likelihood, no more than two EFTA countries will in the end become EU members. The next step will then be to reform the institutions of the European Union. Under this scenario, therefore, Central and Eastern European countries will not have a chance to join the European Union until well into the next century. They would be well-advised to take up Per Wijkman's suggestion to try to join the EFTA in the meantime.

Comment

THORVALDUR GYLFASON

Per Wijkman's paper conveys an urgent message: namely, that EFTA can and should continue to contribute to free trade in Europe by providing a house and home for those European countries that are not yet ready or not willing to join the European Union. In the context of European integration, he views EFTA as a "waiting room" and "training school" for these reluctant countries. EFTA can serve as a bridge between the European Union and the rest of Europe. I agree with Wijkman that this bridge should be kept open. Let me here provide a view from the bridge.

European integration rests on two main pillars: one economic, one political. Economic integration is intended primarily to promote international trade and efficiency. The European Union and EFTA have indeed been important catalysts of trade and growth in Europe over the years, in addition to the GATT, as witnessed by the Single Market Program of 1992, for example. Political integration, on the other hand, is meant primarily to preserve peace in Europe by fostering continued harmonious coexistence and cooperation, particularly between Germany and its neighbors.

On the whole, European integration has thus far been a resounding success, despite recent turbulence in foreign exchange markets and persistent double-digit unemployment in Europe. The fact that five out of seven EFTA countries (all except Iceland and Liechtenstein, as Wijkman points out) have applied or decided to apply for EU membership bears witness to this.

Thorvaldur Gylfason is Professor of Economics, University of Iceland; Institute for International Economic Studies, University of Stockholm; and Centre for Economic Policy Research (CEPR), London.

The European Economic Area (EEA) was originally intended to bridge the gap between EFTA and the European Community by distinguishing economic from political aspects of European integration. It made sense to gain time by separating continued trade liberalization from intensified political union so political controversy would not delay economy progress. Membership in the EEA yields most of the tangible economic gains from free trade within Europe, at the cost—or benefit, depending on your point of view—of minor losses of national sovereignty. For political reasons, however, the people in some EFTA nations may in the end decide not to join the European Union, against the will of their present governments. If so, the EEA may turn out to be a more durable arrangement than originally intended.

The present institutional structure of the European Union, the EEA, and EFTA provides an important opportunity to bring the Central and Eastern European countries into the mainstream of European affairs where they belong. This is the main thrust of Wijkman's argument, and I agree. The importance of rising to this challenge rests on both the economic and political pillars of European integration.

The economic argument is that the Central and Eastern European countries must grow through increased exports, among other things. The expansion of trade through liberalization is a prerequisite for necessary structural reforms and rapid growth in this region. This means that the European Union and EFTA must open their borders to trade with the Central and Eastern European countries, not only in manufacturing goods, but also in agricultural commodities, textiles, and services. Agriculture is especially important here, for two main reasons.

First, farming is relatively more important in Central and Eastern Europe than in Western Europe. Therefore, a takeoff of export-led growth in Central and Eastern Europe requires farm import liberalization in Western Europe and thus a reorganization of the Common Agricultural Policy (CAP) beyond the reforms of May 1992. Second, a further overhaul of the CAP is necessary in any case to reduce the cost to consumers and taxpayers of maintaining the policy in its present form. The additional cost imposed by the entry of Central and Eastern European countries into the European Union in the first (or second) decade of the next century would bankrupt the CAP in its present form.

Therefore, the integration of Central and Eastern Europe into the mainstream of the European economy, and ultimately into the European Union, necessitates a restructuring of the CAP. This is not to say that free markets should be allowed to reign completely unfettered in agriculture. To the contrary, Europe still needs to protect farmers from excessive fluctuations in their incomes and also to ease the transfer of labor and capital from agriculture to other occupations. But, to spend collectively about $1,500 per household per year, or almost 2 percent of Europe's GNP, on sustaining the CAP is unwise and untenable. In Europe, agriculture is a macroeconomic concern and needs to be discussed in the context of macroeconomic policy. Our political leaders must gather courage to confront special interests at home for the benefit of Europe as a whole.

The political argument for bringing the Central and Eastern European countries into the European mainstream seems compelling, too. It is hard to think of a better way to foster democratic development and strong market economies based on decentralized decision making, pluralism, and private property. Therefore, the Central and Eastern European countries should be enabled to become full participants in European integration as quickly as possible.

The potential gains from eliminating remaining inflation differentials and reducing inflation in Europe further through a common currency are certainly important, but they are probably not large in comparison with the gains from further liberalization of trade, especially in agriculture, as is necessary to achieve an integrated Europe, peaceful and prosperous for a long time to come.

To succeed, however, we must find a way to create jobs in Europe. Persistent double-digit unemployment should direct attention to the structure and functioning of labor markets.

Experience seems to indicate that decentralized labor markets—for instance, in Japan, the United States, and Switzerland—are by and large better-suited to generating high employment and low inflation than highly regulated monopolistic or oligopolistic labor markets of the European type, other things being equal. The problem here concerns externalities and spillover effects. In Europe, wages and work conditions are commonly negotiated by nationwide labor unions and employer associations and are tightly regulated by law. When centralized wage negotiations cover an overwhelming part of the labor force (over 75 percent in nearly all European countries except Switzerland; see Layard, Nickell, and Jackman 1991, 52), unions will bargain directly or indirectly over wages for large and diverse groups of workers. Some workers are employed in well-run, efficient, and profitable firms that are able to pay high wages. Others do their jobs perhaps in poorly run, inefficient, and unprofitable enterprises that cannot afford to pay such high wages. As long as trade unions and employers conduct wage negotiations collectively or at the industry level rather than at the level of the firm, the wage demands of one group of workers can jeopardize the jobs of other groups. In short, this is how in Europe "insiders" can price "outsiders" out of work.

Centralized bargaining about wages has led to considerably less wage dispersion in Europe than is prevalent, say, in the United States, where only about one-eighth of the labor force is unionized, or in Japan, where bonuses on top of negotiated basic wages create scope for considerable wage differentials. To take an extreme example, the wages of 18- and 19-year-olds in Sweden rose from 55 percent of those in the 35–44 age group in 1968 to 80 percent in 1986 (Lindbeck et al. 1993). It is hardly surprising, then, that unemployment in Sweden has increased most dramatically among young and unskilled workers. Not only that, the attempted equalization of the wage structure seems actually to have accentuated income inequalities by throwing many young people out of work.

This anomaly is not the consequence of misguided legislation, but rather the outcome of free negotiations between labor unions and employer associations. This is the sort of thing that tends to happen when prices are set centrally. Indeed, the centralized system of wage formation in Europe today has important elements in common with pricing practices in the former centrally planned economies of Central and Eastern Europe: organized from the center and tightly regulated by law—and all in the name of equality.

We may thus face an unpleasant choice between unemployment and inequality in Europe. We may hope to accept wider wage differentials in order to make some of the unemployed employable. If we do, Europe must reform the arrangements and institutions that have produced the excessively compressed wage structure, which has amplified and exacerbated the unemployment problem. In essence, the labor market ought to function more like other markets, where prices and costs basically equate supply and demand, and without encroaching upon the rights of ordinary working people—rights that are due, in large measure, to the efforts of labor unions over many years.

The European Monetary System was established in the belief that real phenomena such as unemployment are essentially independent of nominal arrangements such as exchange rate regimes. But unemployment in Europe has nonetheless increased incessantly under this system since its inception in 1979. Perhaps the interaction between labor markets and the monetary system was instrumental in increasing unemployment in Europe. One also may suspect that real and nominal rigidities in European labor markets, by preventing real wages and related costs from falling during recessions and by thus destroying jobs, may exert irresistible pressure on governments to inflate their currencies. If so, to put it bluntly, we may face a choice between strong currencies and strong labor market organizations.

Consider the United States. When things go badly in Texas, workers move to California and find jobs there, and vice versa. Americans move across state borders every third year on average. Roughly speaking, about two-thirds of the dynamic adjustment to adverse regional shocks in America involves labor migration, and one-third occurs through real wage reductions (Blanchard and Katz 1992). Compare this with Europe. A Dane who loses his job does not move to Portugal if he does not know Portuguese. A common language may thus be a prerequisite for a successful common currency. Without the same language, and therefore with no place else to go, jobless workers may be stuck at home during recessions.

The prospect of a common currency in Europe thus increases the need to reform labor market institutions and arrangements in Europe to help create conditions for full employment, price stability, and rapid growth. But that will not be easy. Labor market issues, like agricultural ones, tend to be charged with emotion. Even so, economists and central bankers cannot allow their analyses and advice to be unduly restrained by political expediency or special interests.

References

Blanchard, O. J., and L. F. Katz. 1992. "Regional Evolutions." *Brookings Papers on Economic Activity* 1: 1–61.

Layard, R., S. Nickell, and R. Jackman. 1991. *Unemployment: Macro-economic Performance and the Labour Market.* Oxford University Press.

Lindbeck, A. P. Molander, T. Persson, O. Petersson, A. Sandmo, B. Swedenborg, and N. Thygesen. 1993. "Options for Economic and Political Reform in Sweden." *Economic Policy* 17 (October).

5

Austria in a New Europe

HELMUT KRAMER

Austria has not actively participated in the opening and liberalization of Central and Eastern Europe during the past five years. Nor has Austria, having been outside the European Community, contributed to the establishment of the single market within the Community. More than any other country, however, Austria has felt the reverberations of the dramatic economic and political changes on the European continent. These historic transformations have prompted Austria to reassess its strengths and weaknesses, in political and social as well as economic terms, and its role in Europe. This reassessment coincides with Austria's application and recent negotiations to join the European Union.

Austrians, perhaps out of a certain nostalgia for the prominence of the Austro-Hungarian Empire, fancy the notion that their country has a distinctive role on the international stage. They suggest that their national model of social cooperation on economic development might inform economic policymaking abroad, for example, and that Austria might act as a special point of contact for the West vis-à-vis Central and Eastern Europe. While Austria does indeed have things to offer, it tends to exaggerate the importance of these benefits in internal discussions over its future relationship to Europe.

This chapter discusses Austria's extraordinary development during the postwar period and its embeddedness in the European economy. The essay then examines the Austrian model of economic policymaking and social cooperation and the model's relevance to the countries of Central

Helmut Kramer is Director of the Austrian Institute for Economic Research in Vienna.

and Eastern Europe. The chapter assesses Austria's attractiveness as a location of production of tradeable goods and services and then the economic and political issues raised by Austria's prospective entry into the European Union.

Postwar Economic Development

After World War II and the ratification of the Austrian Treaty of 1955, Austria became a neutral country in the heart of a divided Europe, with the Iron Curtain skirting its eastern border. The Austrian economy reoriented itself toward the West and opened its domestic market to increasing external competition. In doing so, Austria progressively adapted to the rules and norms of international economic regimes in tandem with other Western countries.

The new position of Austria in European politics and economics carried unexpectedly positive benefits. Not only did Austria overcome backwardness in economic terms—in most but not all instances, becoming one of the most advanced Western European nations—but its political and economic system functioned in some respects even better than that of many comparable neighbors.

Let me illustrate this assertion with a few indicators. Austrian value added per employee in manufacturing surpassed that of West German industry in the early 1990s, whereas 20 years earlier it lagged behind by 30 percent. During the same two decades, the Austrian market share of OECD world exports rose from 1.3 to 1.7 percent and that of OECD Europe world exports from 2.1 to 2.6 percent—that is, by roughly one-quarter.

GDP per capita at current prices and exchange rates surpassed that of the EC average in 1992 by 19 percent. Measured in purchasing power parities, however, it was nearly equal to the EC average, raising questions of the adequacy of the domestic price level and the intensity of competition or the exchange rate. Additional data on Austria's long-term economic performance and how it compares to the 12 members of the Community are shown in table 1.

Austria was able to catch up with the rest of Europe in the postwar period in part because of a favorable internal social and political environment but also to a large degree because of the postwar international environment. Austria chose with foresight from among a number of strategic options available in the late 1940s and the early 1950s.

This experience does not appear to be directly applicable, for example, to all the problems that the reform countries in Central and Eastern Europe now face. There are many differences in their respective situations. Nevertheless, there are some appealing parallels that will be discussed later.

Table 1 Austria: long-term economic performance, 1972–92
(percentages)

Indicator	EC-12		Austria	
	1972–82	1982–92	1972–82	1982–92
Growth of real GDP (average annual)	+2.3	+2.5	+2.6	+2.5
Share of total fixed capital formation in GDP	+21.9	+19.8	+26.1	+23.6
Growth of real exports of goods and services (average annual)	+4.5	+5.0	+6.0	+5.1
Consumer prices (average annual)	+11.8	+5.3	+6.4	+3.0
Net household savings as share of disposable income	+15.7	+12.5	+9.6	+11.1
General government financial balance as share of GDP	–3.5	–4.2	–1.8	–2.9
Standardized unemployment rate	5.6	9.9	1.7	3.5
Current account balance as a share of GDP	–0.3	0.1	–1.7	0.1

To understand both the parallels and differences, one must examine the factors that led to Austria's success. At the end of the war, a sellers' market prevailed in the world economy; today a buyers' market must be reckoned with for many products, from agricultural to industrial goods. Anyone possessing production capacity in the late 1940s and early 1950s was easily able to sell products at home and abroad.

The Marshall Plan assistance in the Austrian case decisively advanced a sustained period of economic development, and Austria was among the relatively most favored beneficiaries of the European Recovery Programme. Yet its acceptance of this assistance did not imply that Austria was forced to acquiesce in harmful structural distortions. In the early 1950s the country rightly decided to expand its abilities to produce raw materials and semifinished goods that could earn foreign exchange sufficient to import machinery and technology from abroad. This pattern continued into the 1960s.

An important condition for receiving Marshall Plan aid was the opening of the domestic market, which had been sheltered by all sorts of trade barriers after its prewar economic crisis, to foreign competition. Despite having been pursued for the whole postwar period and having culminated in the Austrian application for membership in the European Community in 1989, this strategy has met with some reluctance on the part of Austrian producers and unions. Consequently, market opening has been a decidedly slow, step-by-step process.

In the 1950s, Austria declined to join the European Economic Community, owing to its foreign policy neutrality, which was enshrined in the Austrian Treaty.[1] But, in addition to the imperative of safeguarding neutrality, a desire to avoid the full force of competition from trading partners in Western Europe also discouraged Austrian participation in the Community. In the 1990s, Austria now has a second chance to enter the European Union.

Austrian governments have nonetheless been forward-looking in opting for a policy of international economic openness, which has exposed the domestic economy to formidable foreign competition. Austria became a member of the GATT, the IMF, and the OECD, accepting the obligations thereof. Austria was also a cofounder of EFTA, a partial substitute for membership in the European Community, in 1957. The free trade agreement under EFTA became effective in 1972. The government's hard-currency approach, which virtually pegged the Austrian schilling to the Deutsche mark, was adopted in stages after 1972. Although Austria was not an EC member, it established full convertibility of the schilling in line with EC directives in November 1991.

This market opening contributed not only to a remarkable record of domestic stability of costs and prices but also stimulated innovation and the restructuring of productive capacity. Market opening was consonant with a reasonable balance in the current account except during some shorter periods, such as the second half of the 1970s, in which the adaptation of domestic incomes policy and/or industrial restructuring failed to mesh with the ambitious market-reform goals.

The Austrian Model of Economic Policymaking

The extraordinary success of the Austrian economy in the postwar period owes much to Austria's particular model of economic decision making. The so-called social partnership model includes trade unions and employers in the policymaking process in addition to government and places a premium on maintaining social consensus. As such the postwar Austrian model is very different from, and indeed opposed in some respects to, the prewar Austrian school of economics associated with Friedrich Von Hayek. This section describes the Austrian model and then

---

1. The European Community, unlike other international economic organizations such as the European Free Trade Association (EFTA), the General Agreement on Tariffs and Trade (GATT) and the Organization for Economic Cooperation and Development (OECD), held ambitions to political union. Most of its members, moreover, were also members of NATO.

addresses two questions: what elements of the model might serve economic policymaking in other countries, and to what extent would the model have to be adapted or abandoned with Austrian membership in the European Union?

The use of monetary, fiscal, and incomes policy that emerged during the 1970s by experiment rather than by design, and is now referred to as the Austrian model, has been discussed at length by other authors (e.g., Robinson and Suppanz 1972; Scharpf 1991, 56–69). I do not intend to repeat these treatments here. Many central aspects of this model, however, were abandoned during the 1980s as a result of the strong international influences on the small, open Austrian economy. Among these influences was the shift in basic economic paradigms held by governments of the advanced industrial countries, from the post-Keynesian consensus to a new macroeconomics. This shift was accompanied by a diminishing interest within industrial countries in "Austrian" (as well as "Swedish") solutions for the problems of economic development.

This shift might in part explain the observation that the Austrian example for transformation has often been mentioned in the discussion of approaches toward the transition of Eastern countries but seldom applied. Prescriptions put forward by Austrian scholars have not been put into practice in neighboring countries; instead these countries have tended to orient themselves toward solutions worked out at Harvard or the University of Chicago.

Yet the Austrian system of economic policymaking has persistently succeeded in coordinating a range of fiscal, monetary, and incomes policy in order to ensure macroeconomic stability under difficult external conditions. In autumn 1993, a cut in income taxes was announced (effective as of January 1994), which was—among other goals—intended to reduce wage claims. This in turn was meant to bring moral suasion to bear on producers and public service providers to slow down price increases. The stabilizing influences of microeconomic and macroeconomic policies have permitted interest rate levels even below those prevailing in Germany, despite the fixed exchange rate of the Austrian schilling with the Deutsche mark. Elements of the Austrian approach to economic and social policy may be adopted in situations where the application of pure market principles leads to growing political uneasiness.

The Austrian approach to economic policymaking, in my view, contains a number of basic elements. First, Austrian politics has, consciously or not, always stressed identification of sound principles and aims realized through flexible, pragmatic means. This approach is undogmatic, and it has the advantage of placing added value on a willingness to learn and to adjust. Most important, it obviates delays in making decisions. During the persistent search for the best solutions, the opportunity for adopting the second-best approach is not missed.

Second, the high degree of economic policy effectiveness in Austria is linked with the degree of power concentration in the hands of a few economic agents: Trade Union Congress, Federal Chamber of Industry, central bank, and federal government. A very instructive exposition of the political scene and sociological prerequisites, still valid with some minor caveats, may be found in Robinson and Suppanz (1972).

Undoubtedly, concentrating decision making is simpler in a small, cohesive country. Yet this system would have hardly produced the same results if decisions were left to academics. Typically in Austria, the decision makers, while having a competent brain trust at their disposal, have enough practical experience to know what is politically feasible and how far they can go in a specific case. This up to now has obviated populist reversals. The recession of 1992–93 and the growing exposure not only to imports of low-cost products but also to the immigration of workers from Eastern Europe no doubt have challenged these balancing skills.

Third, Austrian policy tends to bring demand-side and supply-side instruments into play simultaneously. One of the hallmarks of what came to be known as Austro-Keynesianism was that it used macroeconomic demand management via the state budget merely as one tool among several for the attainment of overall economic aims. Thus, what amounted to the rediscovery of the supply side in other countries in the 1980s was not new in Austria.

Fourth, macroeconomic stabilization is not imposed solely through the public budgets. It must at all times be flexibly augmented by monetary, incomes, industrial, and foreign trade policies. A multiple-instrument approach reduces risk and prevents overly abrupt changes in the economic performance. It is expedient to combat inflationary tendencies by restrictive monetary policy. But efforts to bring down inflation might also be reinforced by the pressure of international competition.

Internal stability has been safeguarded not by money-supply rule but by means of an external anchor—the stable exchange rate against the Deutsche mark—and by social mechanisms designed to orient incomes policy to the exchange rate. The adoption of this external target and internal adaptation to it developed after experimentation with exchange rate baskets in the 1970s. As the German monetary authorities have always subscribed to a policy that gives internal stability high priority in economic policy decisions, Austria not only had a fixed exchange rate for about half of its external transactions but was also able to import stability.

This means that the domestic economy was forced to adapt to external conditions and that in some sense economic policy decisions are in effect made beyond its borders. Given Austria's size and location, such a situation is not surprising. For Austria's instrumental policy mix to work, its domestic cost and price levels must be more or less in line with those in Germany. Austria's unions and businesses have over the years become accustomed in wage negotiations to considering at least the cost competitiveness of the exposed sector—in other words, they have accepted the fixed exchange rate. Wage increases were considerably higher over quite a long period in the 1980s and 1990s than they were in Germany. But labor productivity growth was also higher and unit labor costs in industry have thus declined in Austria compared with Germany since 1987.

Fifth, tax policy has in recent years become a more prominent tool of the Austrian model. Out of increased concern about international competitiveness, a topic discussed in greater depth below, tax policy has been used to enhance the attractiveness of the country as a production site. Corporate earnings are now taxed at a rate of 34 percent, which is considerably lower than that of most European countries, especially neighboring Germany. Reforms of financial market institutions have also been brought to bear on the competitiveness problem.

The Austrian model, in my view, does indeed contain useful lessons for the countries of Central and Eastern Europe. Two lessons, which stem from the supply-side elements of the model, seem particularly applicable:

- Grant preferential fiscal treatment with respect to investments as opposed to consumption. For a long time, Austria granted accelerated depreciation to taxpayers, and savings promotion remains part of the Austrian fiscal system. These measures are sensible because reform economies lack sufficient foreign capital. Foreign direct investment and foreign lending can be expected to finance at most a fraction of the needed investment projects. In Eastern Europe, the bulk of these funds have to be provided through forgone consumption.

- Mobilize savings for the renovation of houses and apartments, even if there are "gray" markets that would profit thereby. This stabilizes personal living conditions, serves as a visible sign to the populace that progress is being made, builds confidence in the economy and—because of low import requirements—improves the balance of payments on the current account.

The answer to the second question—to what extent would membership in the European Union require changes in economic policymaking in Austria—is that the model will have to be adapted but need not be abandoned. For example, if Austria accedes to the Union, the convergence criteria of the Maastricht Treaty theoretically could restrict the flexible application of fiscal policy. But Austria's fiscal deficits and government debt are low relative to the European average. The schilling has been pegged to the D-mark for nearly 15 years without a "realignment." Owing to this demonstrated commitment to exchange rate stability, Austria is well-positioned to be a member of the hard core of the

European monetary union and could qualify without changing this aspect of the Austrian model. Further ramifications of EU membership are discussed below.

Austria as a Location for Production

Austria's growth and stability has been outstanding over a long period. Now that Austria has caught up with the wealthiest and most productive economies, new strategies must be considered. As a leading country, Austria is no longer able to rely on the importation of technology and know-how, as it did during the period of catching up. Indeed, Austria's growth in the last decade has been no better than that of the 12 Community members.

The fundamental changes in the international environment Austria encounters today entail additional opportunities as well as new risks. The internal market of the European Union and the opening of Central and Eastern Europe provide easier access to huge markets and offers new locations for production facilities. But, of course, these new opportunities also entail increased competition.

Austria is debating, as are many other Western European countries, whether it remains an attractive location for the production of goods and services. This debate has been stimulated by several recent developments.

First, the completion of the internal market (Project 1992) is diminishing the comparative advantage of Austria, as it is not yet an EU member. This can be observed very markedly in the shift of foreign direct investment in favor of some (but not all) EC regions and away from nonmembers. Austria has been very adversely affected by this shift. Also, the end of communist rule in Eastern Europe has likewise put an end to Austria's comparative advantage as a neutral country to serve as an intermediary in trade with the Eastern bloc.

Second, costs for major domestic production factors such as labor or the use of natural resources have been rising for quite some time— measured in terms of a common currency—more rapidly than the European average. But these increases have been roughly matched by above-average productivity gains.

Third, as mentioned above, the liberalization of trade in Central and Eastern European countries means that they are now increasingly able to enter Western markets and that they must do so. Their major advantages are low costs of labor and low environmental standards (although their unusually low energy costs are being raised as their generous production subsidies are being greatly reduced). The Czech Republic and Hungary are particularly competitive. This, together with the revaluation of the Austrian currency in effective terms after the unraveling of the European Monetary System (EMS) in 1992–93, has deteriorated the cost competitiveness of at least some sectors of the Austrian economy. This situation must be expected to continue for some years.

Finally, there are other deficiencies in the competitive position of Austria, although the importance of these deficiencies in a comparison with competitors would be hard to assess. There are substantial bureaucratic obstacles to investment in Austria. The country suffers from narrow capital markets. There is a misallocation of educational resources in Austria as well.

In my opinion the most fundamental problem with Austria as a production location is the widespread public skepticism of the benefits of open markets and the weighty requirements high-income production imposes: open-mindedness rather than defensiveness, willingness to take calculated risks (such as new-technology adoption) as opposed to risk-aversion, and flexibility of institutions and income expectations rather than rigidity.

The analysis and forecast of the possible development of Eastern Europe and hence of the future division of labor in this region is a daunting, yet necessary, challenge for economists. Given the breadth of this challenge, economic models are basically insufficient to give reliable answers, especially when they disregard the politics of economic reform. Nonetheless, owing to the rapidly increasing political concern about the seemingly unbeatable cost advantages of Austria's Eastern neighbors, particularly their very low labor costs, the Austrian Institute for Economic Research (WIFO) has taken a first stab at making these calculations to facilitate political decision making.

We started with an adaptation of the Collins-Rodrik model to the Austrian situation (Collins and Rodrik 1991).[2] On the domestic market of Austria as well as on Austrian export markets, we estimated displacement effects of Austrian products in the magnitude of some 6 percent of the output of Austrian manufacturing sectors and a loss of about 50,000 jobs as a result of increased competition from the East. On the export side—under cautious assumptions on shrinking Austrian market shares—similar calculations lead us expect an 8 percent increase in Austrian exports, equivalent to some 60,000 to 65,000 jobs. The net effect would therefore be slightly positive for both the trade balance and employment. Indeed, although the producers of Central and Eastern Europe are a source of low-cost imports, Austrian exports to Central European neighbors since 1989 have increased significantly—more rapidly than Austrian imports from this region.

---

2. We acknowledge weaknesses with this approach. One is the implicit assumption that Eastern European economies would have been able to develop like Western European economies if they had been managed on the basis of market mechanisms and would have benefited from integration agreements and trade liberalization.

These findings predict the opposite result from those of the Collins-Rodrik analysis regarding future bilateral trade. Collins and Rodrik forecast a decline in Austria's trade shares with the East, particularly for Austrian exports to Poland and Hungary. However, Austria has actually reinforced its previously strong position on these markets since 1989. The greater familiarity of Austrian enterprises with Central and Eastern Europe may have given them a lead, at least for a short period. This market position might be defended, even though other Western suppliers are aware of the possibilities offered by Eastern markets. Although the Austrian share of exports to Central and Eastern Europe is high relative to that of other Western countries, it is still smaller than its share during the interwar period (Hochreiter 1989).

Despite the improvement of Austria's balance of payments with the Eastern region, concern about Austrian competitiveness has fueled the public debate. Theories of the political economy of trade explain this phenomenon by the political power of special interest groups, by an asymmetric attitude toward the losses and gains of income and jobs from trade, by public-choice problems, and by free-riding and prisoner's dilemma situations.

Advocates of market mechanisms must, in my opinion, introduce some additional variables into their models. Smooth adaptation to new political or economic conditions may be time-consuming. The change of the European political landscape has come unexpectedly and dramatically. In such a situation, imbalances in many markets have caused drastic shifts in competitive position and therefore in the location of production, which could not be sustainable under medium-term equilibrium conditions. Leaving market forces completely uncontrolled could mean the loss of physical and human capital that could become competitive under a longer time horizon. Under such conditions and after very careful evaluation, transitory and limited protection against product dumping in certain sectors might be advisable. This should in no case succor protectionist tendencies, which could be detrimental for a small open economy, not only because of the resulting delays in inevitable adaptations but also because of the danger of the trading partners taking reciprocal measures.

Although Austria has lost at least some of her former strength as a site for the production of many industrial goods, especially labor-intensive goods or raw materials, some of Austria's traditional strengths remain and are even reinforced by the new environment. Among them I would count some elements of Austria's basic economic philosophy; the climate of social relations; the hard-currency approach and its consequences; the existence of a broad, innovative, and efficient medium-sized enterprise sector; the satisfactory capacity of the infrastructure; and in recent years the tax policy. These advantages seem to have attracted many foreign subsidiaries, not so much to produce goods in Austria, but to use Austria as a base for their Central European activities.

Membership in the European Union

In the summer of 1989, the Austrian government decided to apply for full membership in the European Community, a decision made after a careful review of the effects of Mikhail Gorbachev's *perestroika* on neutral countries. An evaluation of the European Commission's white paper of 1985 on the completion of the internal market added further weight to the decision to apply. At this time, the main arguments for EC membership were on the economic side rather than the political. By forming the internal market, the Community, intentionally or not, would effectively discriminate against outsiders by removing nontariff barriers to trade among all its members. And, furthermore, the Community several times showed its ability and its inclination to protect inside producers when the internal market was disrupted—a tendency harmful for Austrian suppliers of steel or agricultural products.

The argument to join the Community was not so much to gain immediate profits from its economic potential but to avoid the disadvantages of the outsider that depends on its markets—as is the case with Austria, which sells about two-thirds of its exports there.

In view of the political shocks that came in the aftermath of the Eastern European revolutions of 1989–90, Austria also recognized that the Community might provide political shelter to a country in the immediate vicinity of these tensions.

The Austrian application was politely welcomed by the European Community, but many considered Austrian membership as a possible obstacle to deepening EC institutions. Therefore, the Community advocated the formation of the European Economic Area (EEA), extending the core of the internal-market rules to most of the EFTA countries. Although it became effective as of January 1994, the EEA seems only second-best to most EFTA countries as a means of maintaining nondiscriminatory access to the EU markets. In terms of trade policy, the EEA consists basically of a free trade agreement that fails to lift border controls and rules of origin between EU and EFTA countries, though it introduces a common competition policy that provides freedom of movement of services, labor, and capital. Furthermore, agricultural and monetary policy is excluded from the scope of areas the EEA covers.

In the meantime, most other partners in the EFTA have also recognized the consequences of the changed external conditions after the collapse of the Soviet system. Finland, Sweden, Switzerland, and Norway followed Austria with requests for full membership. Formal negotiations opened early in 1993, with a parallel procedure between the Community and Austria, Sweden, Finland, and Norway, respectively. The bulk of EU laws on competition in goods and service markets as well as in the capital and labor markets have already been transformed into national law by Austria and the other applicants, consistent with EEA rules.

Full membership in the European Union requires important additional adaptations, mainly in trade and agricultural policy, and subscription to the goals of European Economic and Monetary Union (EMU) as well as of the political union agreed upon by the 12 members in the Maastricht Treaty.

In the case of Austria, there are tricky issues in the negotiations on the economic as well as on the political levels. The relatively strong macroeconomic performance of Austria—with its above-average GDP per capita and below-average unemployment—indicates that the country will be a net contributor to the EU budget. The net contribution will initially amount to between $1 billion and $1.5 billion a year. But this also means Austria cannot claim a need for permanent exemptions from possibly uncomfortable EU rules. One goal of the Austrian negotiators is to reach agreement on transitional concessions in cases where an immediate application of EU rules would shock sheltered firms, especially in some agricultural products.

The GATT round has made more difficult the harmonization of the national agricultural policy with the Common Agricultural Policy (CAP). Although Austria's agriculture suffers from many of the same problems as Western European agriculture in general, the Austrian situation is aggravated by local producer prices for leading products such as grain and milk that are still higher than the prices set within EU markets. Even competition in the sheltered EU market will be too severe for many Austrian producers. Therefore, Austria can expect a $1 billion loss in income, resulting in the closure of many farms and in claims on the government budget for income transfers to the farmers.

Nevertheless, Austrian farm representatives have subscribed to EU membership in principle because they realize that—in view of the new GATT rules and possibly expanding exports from Eastern Europe—there is no serious alternative to joining the common market. Otherwise farmers risk being partly excluded from it, possibly resulting in a still greater loss of income.

The acceptance of EU trade policy and the common external tariff are also issues that have been raised in negotiations. The autonomous Austrian tariff is on average somewhat higher than the common EU tariff. The Austrian tariff for example, imposes higher rates on imports of textiles and clothing but allows greater access to imports of investment goods and automobiles. More important in principle is the fact that Austria's autonomous free trade agreements and preferences for Eastern European products will be replaced by agreements that exist between the European Union and the countries of Central and Eastern Europe. The contents of new free trade rules that EFTA countries negotiated with the Central and Eastern European countries are roughly similar to the Europe treaties between the latter and the European Union; thus no serious problem is foreseen on this issue.

There is widespread concern in Austria that formal adoption of EU environmental rules, or a greater emphasis on use of market forces to protect the environment, could result in a possible relaxation of the comparatively ambitious Austrian ecological standards. Similarly, there is opposition to abolishing restrictions on road traffic crossing the Austrian Alps, the bulk of which travels from North to South and threatens increased traffic congestion and pollution. The European Union argues that former transit traffic would become internal traffic upon Austria's entry into the Union and therefore should not be subject to restrictions.

There are a number of estimates on the macroeconomic effects on the Austrian economy of entry into the European Union. Many of them may be countered by arguments made in the aftermath of the Cecchini report. The main source of contention lies in how to evaluate the benefits of the dynamic scale economies of the bigger market and its common policies. In the case of a new entrant, furthermore, such an evaluation should also quantify the value of possible discrimination and the improvement in influence on EU policy decisions—a nearly impossible task. The overwhelming majority of studies nevertheless suggest that anything less than full membership would result in growing long-term disadvantages for the Austrian economy. Alternative strategies such as an improvement of economic links with Eastern Europe or with overseas regions could not wholly offset these disadvantages.

In light of the unification of Germany and fears of German predominance in Europe, the entry of Austria into the European Union would seem to have the further benefit of contributing to a more balanced set of economic relations. The abolition of nontariff barriers of all sorts would encourage Austrian entrepreneurs to venture into markets other than the one with which Austrians are most familiar: Germany. The incentive for Austria to diversify its economic relations within Europe will be accentuated, moreover, by the realization that the German economy may not be as dynamic as Europe would wish in the foreseeable future.

At least in economic terms, Austria's links with countries outside Europe has never been very intense (tables 2 and 3). This is still true, even if in recent years the presence of Austrian goods and companies in Asian as well as American markets has increased from previously very low levels. Austria has also taken steps toward commercial engagement with developing countries. But again, these steps seem rather tentative—not surprising given the well-known reluctance of the majority of the Austrian population to think globally. Austrian membership in the European Union is all the more important for this reason as well.

Just as Austrian membership in the European Union would change Austria, it will also change the European Union in several important ways. Austrian membership will alter the Union's relationship to Central and Eastern Europe and the prospects for a multispeed monetary union, to choose two examples.

Table 2 Austria: shares in regional trade, 1992 (percentages)

	Exports	Imports
EC	66.1	67.9
EFTA	8.6	6.8
North America	3.2	4.5
Other OECD	2.6	5.3
Eastern Europe	11.6	7.3
OPEC	2.8	1.9
Other Countries	5.1	6.3

Source: Austrian Institute for Economic Research (WIFO) data bank.

In its response to the Austrian application to join the Community, the European Commission recognized that Austrian membership could enlarge the capacity of the Community for understanding Eastern and Southeastern European developments. The Austrian elite—at least in the eastern part of the country—also believes this.

The Austrian economy has already exploited its proximity to the emerging market economies, spreading a network of subsidiaries and joint ventures in Hungary, the Czech Republic, Slovakia, and Slovenia. In these countries, Austrian investments rank among the most numerous of all Western investors. Austrians regard these markets as a sort of enlarged home market for Austrian products and services, despite several remaining tariff and nontariff barriers.

Playing the role of broker between the European Union and the countries of Eastern Europe is not a realistic ambition, however, because most of the latter are inclined to orient themselves toward the dominant forces in the European Union located in Brussels, Paris, Bonn, and London. The capacity of Austrians to act as "interpreters" of Eastern Europe seems to me to be based solely on a common historical and cultural heritage. This heritage may be seen as an obstacle rather than an advantage for the development of special political relations between Austria and these countries.

Nevertheless, there seems to be potential to develop a consistent approach toward closer relations with these countries. Local border-traffic problems, neighborhood and environmental questions, infrastructural networks, and the problem of migration may be tackled efficiently in the framework of the Central European Initiative in which Austria and Italy are the driving forces.

Finally, Austrian entry would expand the number of EU members

Table 3 Austria: shares in imports from the OECD, 1982–92 (percentages)

	1982	1989	1992
EC	1.86	2.27	2.39
EFTA	2.06	2.06	2.02
North America	0.30	0.38	0.37
Other OECD	0.46	0.56	0.75
Eastern Europe	5.35	5.80	7.65

Source: International Monetary Fund, *Direction of Trade.*

that could qualify for membership in the European Monetary Union. Although Austria has not been a member of the EMS, it is the European country that has the longest tradition of conforming to Maastricht-style criteria for economic convergence. Austria could form a European hard-currency bloc with at least Germany, the Netherlands, and France—and Switzerland, if it were to overcome domestic political obstacles and enter the Union as well. The existence of such a bloc would reinforce the multispeed concept of monetary union and increase the likelihood that a subgroup would establish a common currency under the timetable established in the Maastricht Treaty or with a relatively short delay.

The turbulence within the EMS in 1992 and 1993 forced the Scandinavian applicants to the European Union to abandon their tight links to the ECU and D-mark because their internal fiscal situation, costs of production, and price levels were not consistent with the requirements of a fixed exchange rate. These countries might now more carefully study the Austrian experience, in which the hard-currency option has proved a success for more than a decade and a half.

The membership negotiations were completed at the end of February, which will give the European Parliament time to ratify the agreement before adjournment in May. The results of these negotiations must be approved by the Austrian electorate in a referendum, which is scheduled for June 1994. Those issues that are particularly salient for the Austrian electorate include transit traffic and environmental concerns.

It seems appropriate to review the Austrian system of incentives aimed at promoting growth and employment as well as autonomous instruments in the fields of social or environmental policies. The former could clash with the competition policy of the European Union, the latter with the goal of international competitiveness, given the openness of the country and the mobility of capital and qualified labor. The appropriate response would not be to retreat from European integration, but rather to pursue a strategy of maximum support to enterprises by providing an excellent infrastructure and directing more resources to education and training. As these goals can only be reached over a rather long period, the design of a short-term response in the event of a recession will be a challenge to politicians, once protectionist measures are ruled out. It is a challenge Austria confronts together with all its neighbors and partners in an increasingly integrated global economy.

References

Austrian Institute for Economic Research (WIFO), Koordin. K. Aiginger. 1993. *Chancen und Gefährdungspotentiale der Ostöffnung.* Studie, 3 Teile. Wien.

Baldwin, R. E. 1989. "The Political Economy of Trade Policy." *Journal of Economic Perspectives* 3, no. 4 (Fall).

Baldwin, R. E. 1993. *The Potential for Trade between the Countries of EFTA and Central and Eastern Europe.* EFTA Occasional Paper No. 44. Geneva (June).

Beirat für Wirtschafts- und Sozialfragen. 1992. *Ostöffnung.* Studie No.67 (Wien).

Collins, Susan M., and Dani Rodrik. 1991. *Eastern Europe and the Soviet Union in the World Economy.* Washington: Institute for International Economics.

Guger, A. 1993. *Lohnstückkostenposition der Industrie 1992 verschlechtert.* Austrian Institute for Economic Research (WIFO)-Monatsberichte (July) S.387 ff.

Handler, H. 1989. *Grundlagen der österreichischen Hartwährungspolitik.* Wien: Manzverlag.

Hochreiter, E. 1989. *Austria's Role as a Bridgehead Between East and West.* Oesterreichische Nationalbank Working Paper No. 14. Vienna (November).

Kommission der Europäischen Gemeinschaften. 1991. *Stellungnahme zum Beitrittsantrag Österreichs.* Brüssel (Juli).

Kramer, H. 1993. *The Impact of the Opening of the East on the Austrian Economy: A First Quantitative Assessment.* Oesterreichische Nationalbank, Working Paper No. 11. Vienna (March).

Kramer, H. 1991. "Imperfections in the European economic integration: observations from an Austrian viewpoint." In *EFTA countries in a changing Europe.* Geneva: EFTA Secretariat.

Kramer, H. 1992a. "Österreichs Wirtschaft am Vorabend des EG-Beitritts." In A. Khol, G. Ofner, and A. Stirnemann, *Österreichisches Jahrbuch für Politik 1991.* Wien.

Kramer, H. 1992b. *Die Integration Osteuropas in die Weltwirtschaft.* Austrian Institute for Economic Research (WIFO)-Monatsberichte (April), S. 221 ff.

Richter, S., and Stankovsky, J. 1991. *Die neue Rolle Österreichs im Ost-West-Handel.* Studie. Wien: Austrian Institute for Economic Research (WIFO) and Vienna Institute for Comparative Economic Studies (WIIW) (December).

Robinson, D., and H. Suppanz. 1972. *Prices and Incomes Policy: The Austrian Experience.* Paris: Organization for Economic Cooperation and Development.

Scharpf, Fritz W. 1991. *Crisis and Choice in European Social Democracy.* Trans. by Ruth Crowley and Fred Thompson. Ithaca: Cornell University Press.

Seidel H., ed. 1984. *Geldwertstabilität und Wirtschaftswachstum.* Proceedings of a seminar in October 1983 jointly organized by the International Monetary Fund and the Austrian National Bank, Göttingen.

Stankovsky, J. 1992. *Die Direktinvestitionen Österreichs in den Oststaaten.* Austrian Institute for Economic Research (WIFO)-Monatsberichte (August), S. 415ff.

Comment

THOMAS D. WILLETT

Professor Kramer's paper presents a wide-ranging view of the roles of Austria in a new Europe. His task would have been much easier, of course, if it were clearer how the new Europe will evolve, but if anything, the discussions at this conference have increased my perceptions of the uncertainties facing Europe. The push for Economic and Monetary Union in Europe has faced a major temporary if not permanent setback, and grave concerns have been expressed about the outlook both for global trade liberalization and for the entry into the European Union of the current EFTA applicants, including Austria. Thus a liberal economist's joy at the collapse of communism in Europe and the former Soviet Union and the progress of the Community's Single Market Program must be tempered by recognition of the major challenges facing Europe (and the world economy more generally). One of the most crucial challenges for the West is to devise politically feasible ways of facilitating the transition in Central and Eastern Europe. While foreign aid has a role to play, the consensus is that its role will be relatively minor compared with the self-help efforts of the economies in transition. But access to Western markets (on both the export and import sides) is of crucial importance for the economic health of the economies in transition. In overall terms, the Western economies will reap substantial gains from this transformation process as well. As is emphasized in Professor Inotai's paper, however, the comparative advantages of the former centrally

Thomas D. Willett is Horton Professor of Economics at Claremont Graduate School and Claremont McKenna College.

planned economies are heavily concentrated in the so-called politically sensitive industries, which have succeeded in gaining special protection in the West. (This is roughly as true for the United States as it is for Western Europe.)

Professor Kramer's discussion covers both the effects of recent developments in Europe on the Austrian economy and the possible use of Austrian experiences as a role model for policy development in other countries. I would like to try to link these two topics. As Professor Kramer notes, Austria has been especially affected by increased exports from the Czech Republic and Hungary. Producer pressure to limit cheap imports from the formerly centrally planned economies are mounting throughout Europe, at a time when governments are especially prone to succumb to such pressures because of high domestic unemployment rates. At such times, political pressures for protectionism and expansionary macroeconomic policies almost always increase. Neither of these responses is appropriate for most Western European countries, however. While this matter is still the subject of some controversy, most of the authors in this volume support the view that only a small part of the high unemployment facing most Western European countries is due to the Keynesian factor of deficient aggregate demand. Most is due to structural imbalances and impediments to the efficient operation of factor markets (in part caused by the side effects of social legislation). In such circumstances, expansionary fiscal and monetary policies, while likely still to generate some short-term stimulus to employment, will over the medium and longer term result primarily in higher rates of inflation, which will increase uncertainty and lead to decreases in productivity and employment.

Through its long-standing pursuit of a hard-currency strategy, Austria has provided an important practical example of the theoretical predictions of recent macroeconomic analysis, which stresses the importance of following low- rather than high-inflation policies in order to maximize employment and economic performance. As is documented in Professor Kramer's paper and in the study by Anton Kausel (1993), Austria's economic performance over the last several decades has been outstanding. Not only has inflation been low and the growth in real incomes quite favorable, the unemployment rate over the past decade has been substantially below the average for Western Europe. Thus there is good reason for other countries to study the Austrian experience carefully.

Of course, in doing this, it is important to attempt to take into account the role of particular national factors and characteristics, which may influence the effects of particular policy strategies. Thus, for example, while I think the hard-currency peg of the Austrian schilling to the German D-mark has worked extremely well for Austria, drawing upon the theory of optimum currency areas (see, e.g., references and analysis in De Grauwe 1992; Wihlborg and Willett 1991), it may not work equally well in other situations. I would recommend universally, however, Austria's low-inflation objective and its high degree of central bank independence to help achieve this objective.

Another major policy conclusion aptly illustrated by Austria's experience is that sound macroeconomic policies are a necessary but not a sufficient condition for strong economic performance. In recent years, there has been substantially increased recognition in the economics and political economy literature of the important effects that differences in institutional and contractual arrangements can have on the operation of labor markets (see, e.g., the analysis and references in De Grauwe 1992; Willett 1988). Several conference participants made references to the substantially greater growth in employment in the United States than in Western Europe over the past decade or so, and many equated this with differences in the generosity of the social safety nets provided on each continent. I found this especially interesting since only a few weeks before one of my colleagues, Linus Yamane, presented a seminar at Claremont McKenna College focusing on why labor markets appeared to work much better in Japan than in the United States. I raise this point because, while I have no doubt that the overall levels of social benefits provided will have some effect on the behavior of labor markets, I suspect that the ways in which those benefits are provided are likely to be of at least equal importance.

For a wide variety of reasons—including the current levels of unemployment, the need for improving internal adjustment mechanisms for countries that face the loss of exchange rate adjustment options due to monetary union, and the need to adjust to changing comparative advantages such as are being generated by liberalization in historically planned economies—countries must seriously evaluate the institutions that influence their labor and product markets. This should be a cooperative multinational endeavor in which countries seek to learn from each other's experiences. It is not clear to me whether aspects of the social partners approach, which has been practiced with such success between government, unions, and businesses in Austria, can be adapted for use by other countries, but this question is certainly worthy of serious study.

Kramer said that changes in the preferred macroeconomic paradigms on which to base economic policy had diminished international interest in the Austrian approach. I think that this was true for a time, but I believe we are now in the middle of another shift of views: aspects of neoclassical macroeconomics are beginning to coalesce with the recognition of the importance of differences in economic and institutional structures. This new macroeconomics gives us a much sounder basis for analysis, and from this perspective there will be considerable interest in the policy experiences of countries such as Austria and New Zealand. This has certainly been true in the case of my own research (Burdekin et al. 1992; Banaian et al. forthcoming).

As a final point, let me briefly draw a linkage between the papers by Inotai, Kramer, and Wijkman. Austria is especially well-positioned to enter the European Union in that it is one of the few countries for which joining a European currency union would present no major problems. But as several authors have noted in this volume, on other counts joining the Union may not now look nearly as attractive as it did several years ago, and there is a good chance that the necessary public support for entry may be lacking. Austria is well-situated to play a strong role in promoting trade liberalization between EFTA and the Central and Eastern European countries. Professor Kramer notes the strong protectionist pressures within Austria against exports from Central Europe, but this could be a situation where the best defense is a strong offense. A major initiative by the Austrian government to promote increased economic integration between Western and Central and Eastern Europe along one or more of the lines sketched out by Per Wijkman would be highly beneficial in its own right, as well as having the possible additional benefit of challenging domestic advocates of protectionism. Such an initiative would of course carry domestic political risks, but I believe that it is worth serious consideration.

References

Banaian, King, Richard C. K. Burdekin, and T. D. Willett. "On the Political Economy of Central Bank Independence." In Kevin D. Hoover and Steven M. Sheffrin, *Monetarism and the Methodology of Economics: Essays in Honor of Thomas Mayer*. Edward Elger (forthcoming).

Burdekin, Richard C. K., Clas Wihlborg, and T. D. Willett. 1992. "A Monetary Constitution Case for an Independent European Central Bank," *The World Economy* (March): 231–49.

De Grauwe, Paul. 1992. *The Economics of Monetary Integration*. Oxford: Oxford University Press.

Kausel, Anton. 1993. "Four Decades of Success: Austria's Economic Rise within the OECD from 1950 to 1992." *Finanz-nachrichten* (Special issue). Vienna.

Wihlborg, Clas, and T. D. Willett. 1991. "Optimum Currency Areas Revisited." In Clas Wihlborg, Michele Fratianni, and T. D. Willett, *Financial Regulation and Monetary Arrangements After 1992*. Amsterdam: North Holland.

Willett, Thomas D., ed. 1988. *Political Business Cycles*. Durham, NC: Duke University Press.

Comment

ANDREAS KEES

Professor Kramer's paper presents the full spectrum of problems Austria must face when entering the European Union. Some of these problems would arise in an even more difficult context if the country did not enter the Union.

My remarks are threefold. First, I will expand upon two of Kramer's statements. Second, I will link these issues to previous discussion about the institutional consequences. Third, I will deal with the new relationships that EU enlargement creates for the new member states.

Kramer notes a "widespread public skepticism" within Austria regarding the efficiency and benefits of open markets. This attitude presents a great danger and deserves strong corrective action. Second, although accession to the European Union does not preclude transitional arrangements for the new entrants, one should be extremely cautious, even when granting temporary exceptions to EU rules and provisions. Entry into the Union must be used to accelerate structural adjustment.

Austria's role in the new Europe will pose institutional issues for the country itself and for the European Union, as would the entry of the other EFTA countries. In streamlining decision-making procedures, the Union will doubtless have to take into account the interests of the negotiating countries. The institutional reform of the larger European Union cannot take place at the expense of the interests of the smaller countries alone. All member states must contribute in order to benefit from a larg-

Andreas Kees, Secretary of the Monetary Committee (1978–93), is now adviser to the Austrian National Bank.

er and more efficient Union. One of the purposes of the European Union is to avoid the dominance of a single large country or a small group of countries, and this must be respected in the new institutional balance. The European Union is not a hegemon but a commonwealth. Every member has the chance to provide input on its development.

What Austrian membership in the new Europe offers the country outweighs what Austria must contribute in economic and political terms in order to join. The European Union is a cooperative entity that offers its constituent members an added value in terms of performance and perspective. This is the main motivation for joining the Union. The qualitative jump requires—as the other side of the coin—more policymaking responsibility from its members. Only when members accept both the performance benefits and the responsibility will the member countries realize the added value of European Union.

There are countless policy areas where the Union acts in common. All EU-level policies and those guided by the article on subsidiarity bear this potential for common action. The recent growth strategy is also such an opportunity: there is no better possibility for overcoming recession and fighting unemployment. The Union's external commercial policy also offers added value. It would be wrong to see this policy framed according to the lowest common denominator. Gary C. Hufbauer has confirmed in his analysis that the European Union as an entity is more open to the outside than its members would have been if they had acted independently. The value added by membership in the European Union will become most salient when a member country takes up the mantle of the presidency of the Union, at which time it must promote the common rather than the national interest.

Several additional points about the benefits and responsibility of membership should be made. First, the governments and citizens of member states do not naturally accept the new responsbilities associated with membership in the European Union. It takes time for some countries to internalize the responsibilities membership requires. Second, the benefits of membership are not simply related to the size of the European Union. The benefits of membership in the original Community of the Six were not measurably smaller than the benefits of membership in the enlarged European Union. The European Union, its member states, and applicants should resist the seductiveness of power associated with the growth in the size of the membership alone. Finally, national interests will remain the bread and butter of intergovermental bargaining and politics within the European Union. The Treaty on European Union, in particular the principle of subsidiarity embodied therein, impedes a homogenization of the diversity and variety among the member states and regions.

The Union's potential performance benefits cannot be attained if members think in terms of "us" and "them." The treaty reflects this desire to promote an attitude of community. Article 6 forbids discrimination by nationality, and Article 3b defines subsidiarity, which reflects the idea that the whole is greater than the sum of its parts.

New member states must recognize the challenge in this relationship and take up their part of this new task. Member states should ensure that EU policy informs and guides the preparation of national policies. It is not enough to bring one's problems to the Union. One must accept the Union's judgment on how these problems ought to be resolved, even if afterward they are referred back to the national level. All this requires a change of political behavior.

Austria, by virtue of its economic performance and historic ties to East and West, can lead the way in leveling the barriers of European diversity by contributing to the performance benefits that members of the Union share. This should be Austria's role in a new Europe and would be the best answer to the question posed by the title of the conference (on which this volume is based), "Europe: What Next?"

Comment

HEINRICH MATTHES

In his interesting paper, Professor Kramer places rather heavy emphasis on what he sees as Austria's weaknesses in international competition, such as:

- the weakening of its comparative advantages as a raw material producer;

- the fact that Austria is no longer a cheap-labor country;

- the lack of a strong and innovative technological base.

The first two "weaknesses" are characteristic of most highly developed economies and, given the strong growth of productivity in Austria, should not give special cause for concern. Furthermore, as far as labor costs are concerned, Kramer notes that Austria has effective social mechanisms for keeping them under control.

The problem of the technological base and lack of innovation is, of course, a serious one and was identified as such in a recent study by EFTA on the effects of integration into the European Economic Area ("Effects of 1992 on the manufacturing industries of the EFTA countries," April 1992). However, this problem can be overcome, in particular through cooperation between medium-sized firms, which Kramer characterizes as "innovative and efficient," and by cross-border cooperation.

Kramer points out that the EU internal market program has increased

Heinrich Matthes is Deputy Director General, Commission of the European Communities, Economic and Financial Affairs.

the attractiveness for foreign direct investment of some of the EU regions, in part at the expense of Austria. Austria's present disadvantage in this respect is only temporary and should disappear with integration in the EEA and later with membership in the Union.

The EFTA study referred to above concluded that a large part of Austria's manufacturing industry would be affected by the removal of non-tariff barriers in the EEA. The affected sectors account for 43 percent of employment and 38 percent of value added in manufacturing. However, the sectors that were considered to be in a weak position represent only 9 percent of manufacturing employment and value added, while those judged to be in a strong position to benefit from the removal of barriers account for 15 percent of employment and 12 percent of value added.

Increasing integration with the European Union should also lead Austrian businesses to widen their horizons beyond Germany to take advantage of the opportunities that await them in the other member states. Furthermore, with its long-established stable money policy, Austria should experience no special difficulties in moving toward full Economic and Monetary Union.

As for Central and Eastern Europe, Kramer notes that the opening of the economies of these countries has led Western companies to choose Austria as a base for their operations in the region. In addition, Austria's exports to its Eastern neighbors have been growing faster than its imports. Because Austrian businesses generally have closer links than most Western firms with the Central European countries, particularly Hungary, the Czech Republic, and Slovakia, they have better knowledge of their strengths and weaknesses. This knowledge puts Austrian firms in a good position both to take direct advantage of new opportunities in these countries and to act as intermediaries between West and East. In the longer term, enlargement of the European Union to include some or all of the Central European countries should enhance Austria's role still further.

In conclusion, therefore, it seems that the changing configuration of Europe offers important opportunities to Austria. Through the opening of the Iron Curtain, Austria suddenly finds itself returning from the periphery of Europe right into the center. This is per se an advantage. Further advantages arise from entry in the European Union. Both developments are equivalent to huge positive supply shocks for the Austrian economy.

It is thus not surprising that Austrian-model simulations calculated positive real growth effects for Austria from EU membership of around 3.5 percent within six years. The right approach to the present challenge is thus an active forward strategy. The short-term "destruction" of certain old industries is part of the necessary price to be paid for higher welfare in the future. Arguments calling for transitory regimes are quite dangerous and should not be used as an excuse for shifting problems that could be tackled today into the future.

With respect to enhanced competition from its Eastern European neighbors in particular, Austria should resist a protectionist reflex against "unfair" competition from countries with low labor costs and low environmental standards. Austria, more than any other Western European country, has a great interest in the rejuvenation and prosperity of the countries of Central and Eastern Europe. The great temptation now is to react to all these competitiveness challenges by retreating from them. This "easy approach" is a great danger for Austria's future. If, however, Austria reacts positively and takes up these challenges, it will reap the benefits of the progressively deepening international division of labor.

6

Central and Eastern Europe

ANDRÁS INOTAI

The sweeping transformation taking place in Europe is best reflected in the widely publicized framework of bilateral association agreements between the European Union and Central and Eastern European countries. Czechoslovakia, Hungary, and Poland signed agreements in December 1991, followed by Romania and Bulgaria roughly one-and-a-half years later. In the cases of Hungary and Poland, the full agreement came into effect in February 1994. But in the cases of the Czech Republic, Slovakia, Romania, and Bulgaria, only the trade sections of the agreement are in force as of this writing.

The push toward institutionalization of relations between Central and Eastern Europe and the European Union has been driven by the reform countries' three basic expectations. First, with the collapse of the Council for Mutual Economic Assistance (CMEA) and the contraction of domestic markets in Central and Eastern Europe, these countries expected to be able to reorient traditional trade flows to new markets in the West. Although some countries (notably Hungary, and to some extent Poland) started on this path long before the dissolution of the CMEA and the Soviet Union, the massive drive for trade reorientation arose only after 1990. As a result, the European Community became the trade anchor of the transformation process in Central and Eastern Europe.

Second, Brussels has been expected to play a stabilizing role in the transforming region, not only in economic but also in political terms. Intensifying internal problems of the transformation process have underscored the EU's role as security anchor. Potential conflicts among

András Inotai is General Director of the Institute for World Economics in Budapest.

ethnic groups have become actual conflicts, and NATO has been reluctant to fill the security gap that emerged in the "soft area" between the newly unified Germany and the disintegrating Soviet Union. The coup d'etat against Gorbachev played a catalytic role in pushing Brussels to the forefront as a security anchor.[1]

The third expectation, which although underplayed is probably the most important, concerns the overall modernization needs of the Central and Eastern European countries. Because of the growing difficulties of CMEA cooperation, technological backwardness, decreasing competitiveness, and rapidly increasing foreign indebtedness, Hungary and to some extent Poland began to look toward the Community as the modernization anchor of the region in the early 1980s.

This paper cannot cover all three key areas. Because the security aspects are mostly related to noneconomic issues, this paper will focus on an evaluation of the association agreements as the potential trade and modernization anchor for the transforming national economies. The next section offers an overview of the trade developments before 1993 and gives some basic conclusions. The third section portrays the rapidly deteriorating trade environment in 1993 and tries to identify the most important consequences. The fourth section analyzes the fundamental strategic deficiencies of the agreements. The concluding section deals with scenarios and options for the European Union, for Central and Eastern Europe, and for institutionalized cooperation between the two.

Success Story in the Making?

As a result of the dramatic political and economic transformation of Central and Eastern Europe, the European Union has emerged as the main supporting institution in Europe. This new role was very different from the European Community's behavior in the 1970s and 1980s, when the Community stressed political rather than economic relations. Meanwhile, the small and economically vulnerable Central and Eastern European countries stressed their vital economic interests in increased cooperation. EC external economic policy, which developed as a network of bilateral preferential trade agreements, was considered the most important bottleneck: prior to 1988 it discriminated against or at best disfavored Central and Eastern European imports.

After these "treatyless decades," the joint declaration between the European Community and the CMEA in June 1988 opened the way for the bilateral trade and cooperation agreements signed between 1988

---

1. Recent events in Moscow obviously have far-reaching consequences for the security of Central and Eastern Europe. However, these cannot be taken into account in this paper.

Box 1 Generalized System of Preferences

The Generalized System of Preferences (GSP) is a system under which industrial nations give preferential rates of duty on imports from less-developed countries, without receiving trade concessions in return. Usually sensitive products are excluded, and ceilings are set on benefits available to any one country for a specific product.

By granting GSP status to Hungary and Poland as of January 1990, and to Czechoslovakia and Bulgaria as of January 1991, the European Community abolished most tariffs and quotas on manufactured products. Immediately, these "state trading countries" jumped from the bottom of the EC trade policy pyramid to its upper tier. Moreover, the Community extended GSP treatment unilaterally, without concessions from the transforming economies.

However, the GSP rates were not binding and could not be relied upon in making investment decisions. Moreover, some quantitative restrictions imposed on highly sensitive sectors remained in force (e.g., steel, textiles). More importantly, EC rules of origin did not allow for cumulation among the reform countries, nor did the GSP grant tariff exemption to subcontracted exports. Despite these limitations, the GSP system was a qualitative improvement in market access for Central and Eastern Europe.

and 1990.[2] Despite criticism, these documents were considered a success and provided a medium-term policy guideline. But the dramatic events of 1989 and 1990 completely outdated these agreements long before they could be fully implemented.

The new approach of the Community went considerably beyond the scope of the trade and cooperation agreements, which had been so meticulously negotiated. It placed the granting of Generalized System of Preferences (GSP) status to the transforming economies at the center of the new EC philosophy (box 1). Soon, negotiations were initiated to conclude special "Europe agreements," which came to be known as association agreements. Such progress could hardly have been imagined just months before the sweeping changes in Central and Eastern Europe began. Therefore, in historical perspective, the association agreements symbolize a fundamental breakthrough in relations between the two parts of Europe, which followed such different paths after World War II. However, one may ask to what extent this retrospective breakthrough can rightly be considered a prospective breakthrough—one that will provide the right answers at the right time to the burning development and cooperation questions the European continent now faces.

---

2. Romania had concluded a bilateral trade and cooperation treaty with the Community in 1980; however, the purpose of this treaty was more to demonstrate Romania's "sovereign" foreign policy than to secure sizable economic benefits.

Table 1a   Central and Eastern Europe: imports from EC and other areas, 1992 (growth indexes in current dollars, 1989=100)

Importer	EC	Germany[a]	EC without Germany	EFTA	OECD
World	127.7	126.1	128.4	121.1	124.8
Within region	130.5			105.1	121.2
Central and Eastern Europe	171.0	183.7	158.8	102.9	137.0
Former USSR[b]	124.6	144.6	108.7	49.5	92.7
Poland	243.1	222.3	268.3	197.3	220.5
Czechoslovakia	308.7	362.6	241.2	236.8	293.1
Hungary	158.7	154.7	164.0	180.1	167.7
Romania	317.5	274.5	348.6	279.4	256.3
Bulgaria	87.6	71.4	101.4	63.5	78.4

a. German data are for the old Federal Republic of Germany for 1989–90 and for the unified Germany for 1991–92.

b. In 1992, including the Baltic States.

Source: Author's calculations based on *OECD Monthly Statistics of Foreign Trade*, Series A, Paris (January 1992 and August 1993).

The traditionally intra-CMEA trade patterns rapidly switched orientation outward to OECD countries, in particular to the European Community. The EC share in total trade of the Visegrád countries jumped from less than 25 percent in 1989 to about 50 percent in 1992.[3] Thus the Community became the leading trading partner of Central and, increasingly, of Eastern Europe in a short period. Although better market access to the West did not fully offset the market loss suffered in the East, it limited the damage.

Undoubtedly, the newly opened EC market became the engine of export growth for Central and Eastern European countries. Between 1989 and 1992, total Central and Eastern European exports (including the former Soviet states) to the OECD increased by 37 percent and to the European Community by 53 percent, both substantially exceeding the overall import growth of the OECD (21 percent) and of the European Community (30 percent). The export boom was particularly strong for the Central European countries: growth figures were between 62 percent (Hungary) and 121 percent (Czechoslovakia) for exports to the

3. The Visegrád countries—so called because of cooperation bloc agreements concluded at a place of this name near Budapest on 15 February 1991—are the Czech Republic, Hungary, Poland, and Slovakia.

Table 1b Central and Eastern Europe: exports to EC and other areas, 1992 (growth index in current dollars, 1989 = 100)

Exporter	EC	Germany[a]	EC without Germany	EFTA	OECD
World	129.5	151.5	123.0	111.8	120.9
Within region	131.7			105.4	120.6
Central and Eastern Europe	153.2	220.1	119.3	106.1	137.3
Former USSR[b]	131.2	182.3	112.2	82.8	118.3
Poland	208.2	279.5	153.4	128.2	181.6
Czechoslovakia	250.0	351.8	162.2	156.8	221.3
Hungary	178.6	207.5	150.0	150.8	161.6
Romania	64.4	98.5	50.6	78.9	61.6
Bulgaria	194.0	222.6	182.9	143.1	203.0

a. German data are for the old Federal Republic of Germany for 1989–90 and for the unified Germany for 1991–92.

b. In 1992, including the Baltic States.

Source: Author's calculations based on *OECD Monthly Statistics of Foreign Trade*, Series A, Paris (January 1992 and August 1993).

OECD; between 79 percent (Hungary) and 150 percent (Czechoslovakia) for exports to the European Community. In all cases except Bulgaria, growth figures were higher for exports to the Community than to the OECD (table 1).

This development, which even experts had not anticipated, illustrates two points. First, it refuted the frequently expressed view that ex-socialist countries should not be granted better market access because they would not be able to make use of it, given their limitations with respect to technology, quality, and competitiveness. Exactly the opposite proved true. The Central and Eastern European economies were able to compete successfully in Western European markets, provided they were allowed to compete on equal terms with the EC member states.

More importantly, the increase in exports was not due to rapid growth in exports only of select product groups—as was feared by those who argued that Central and Eastern Europe enjoyed greater competitiveness in Western Europe's most sensitive sectors. Certainly, Central and Eastern European industries such as textiles, clothing, steel, and, to a limited extent, agriculture were clearly among the beneficiaries from market opening. However, rather surprisingly, exports across the board, from textiles to machinery, and from steel to petrochemicals, demonstrated dynamic growth.

Part of the region's export success may be explained by the existence of an established industrial structure, which was the result of the autarky of past decades. Other determinants were proximity to Western Europe and the loss of markets in the former CMEA region. But the most important factor was the tremendous wage differences between Western Europe and the former socialist countries. This wage gap, which still prevails, is greater for more highly skilled workers. Thus, the more high-skilled a labor-intensive product is, the greater the wage advantage of Central and Eastern European firms. It is worth noting that while the Visegrád countries accounted for 43 percent of Central and Eastern European exports to the European Community in 1991, their export share ran between 68 and 90 percent for the most technology-intensive and high-skilled labor-intensive product groups (table 2).

Developed-market economies were never before confronted with this kind of challenge. To be sure, the newly industrializing countries of Asia have successfully conquered market shares, but their export offensives were based on a well-defined structural policy with clear export priorities that could be identified in advance. The targeted markets and threatened domestic producers could prepare themselves for the coming test. In addition, sectoral protection was a feasible answer, as new exporters concentrated their advances in selected market segments—for example, steel, autos, or consumer electronics.

Central and Eastern Europe represented a very different challenge. Its export drive between 1989 and 1992 was not based on a well-defined structural policy but resulted from a mixture of long-term comparative advantages and the loss of other markets. No fine-tuned system of import protection, let alone sectoral protection, would have proved adequate to reduce Western Europe's imports of the region's commodities across the board.

It is difficult to assess the role of association agreements in the export successes. The trade sections of the agreements with Romania and Bulgaria came into force only in mid-1993, while those with the Central European countries (Hungary, Poland, the Czech Republic, and Slovakia) have been in force for just 18 months. This is too short a period to draw definitive conclusions.

The agreements with the Visegrád countries took effect during the second half of 1992, while the beginning of their successful export development dates back to 1989. Moreover, the agreements do not include substantial improvements in the market access conditions for GSP products.[4] (For a short description of the main trade measures, see

---

4. On the contrary, some products—mainly textiles and petrochemicals—have been "retariffed" as part of the agreements and now have to face worse market access conditions than under the prior GSP scheme.

Table 2   European Community: imports from Central and Eastern Europe by commodity, 1991 (percent of total EC imports of selected SITC groups)

SITC group	Central and Eastern Europe	Visegrád countries	Share of Visegrád group in Central and Eastern Europe
All commodities	2.81	1.20	43
Food and live animals	2.27	1.88	83
Meat	3.76	3.48	93
Vegetables and fruits	2.95	2.54	86
Raw materials	4.52	1.97	44
Mineral fuels	11.04	0.83	8
Chemicals	1.86	1.18	63
Organic chemicals	2.40	1.61	67
Medicines	0.47	0.35	75
Fertilizers	12.50	5.91	47
Explosives	1.69	1.57	93
Manufactured goods	3.05	1.73	57
Textiles	1.53	1.22	80
Iron and steel	3.97	2.33	59
Manufactures of metal	2.07	1.84	89
Machinery and transportation equipment	0.79	0.54	68
Power generators	1.05	0.79	75
Specialized machinery	1.13	0.99	87
Metalworking machinery	2.13	1.58	74
Electrical machinery	1.05	0.87	83
Automobiles	0.80	0.41	51
Other manufactures	2.41	1.79	74
Sanitary, plumbing, etc.	2.06	1.84	89
Furniture	6.03	3.70	61
Luggage and handbags	2.92	2.47	85
Apparel	4.22	3.23	77
Footwear	3.97	3.13	79

SITC = Standard International Trade Classification.

Source: Author's calculations based on *OECD Trade by Commodities Trade by Commodities,* Series C, Paris, 1991.

Box 2 Trade measures in the association agreements

The trade philosophy underlying the association agreements is based on the asymmetric elimination of, or reduction in, tariffs and the immediate lifting of quantitative restrictions (QRs). Generally, the European Union will carry out this task in five years while the transforming countries have to fulfill the same degree of liberalization within eight to ten years. The schedule of tariff elimination includes manufactured products only, which are classified in three categories. The original time schedule for tariff reductions was slightly modified at the Copenhagen EC summit in June 1993. These are some of the specific tariff and quota commitments:

- EU tariffs on nonsensitive industrial products, which affect about half of total Central and Eastern European exports to the European Union, were eliminated when the trade sections of the agreements entered into force (for the Visegrád countries, on 1 March 1992).

- EU tariff-free quotas, supplemented by lower tariffs for goods over the quota limit, apply to some selected manufactured goods such as chemicals, electronic products, vehicles, and footwear. The tariffs on imports below the quota limit will be eliminated by the end of 1994.

- Tariffs on iron and steel and on textiles and clothing will be abolished by the end of 1995 and 1996, respectively.

- Inputs imported from the European Union that are used in textile subcontracting are exempt from tariffs.

- There is no "asymmetry in time" for liberalizing agricultural trade. Instead, asymmetry is expressed as different speeds at which agricultural tariffs are reduced and quotas for some agricultural goods are increased. The European Union will reduce its tariffs and levies on agricultural goods by 20 percent annually over the next three years and its QRs by 10 percent per year over the next five years. The transforming countries commit themselves to cut their agricultural tariffs by 10 percent annually while increasing agricultural imports from the Union by 5 percent per year over the corresponding period.

The agreements also include new trade rules, which widen the scope for implementing safeguard clauses in the case of a market disturbance, or a critical situation in certain market segments, or a balance of payments problem. Finally, rules of origin stipulate 50 to 60 percent local content; inputs imported from the European Union and the Visegrád countries are considered part of local content.

box 2.) In fact, the main relevance of the agreements is that they institutionalized the GSP scheme. Therefore, one can rightly conclude that the dynamic export development of Central and Eastern Europe was fundamentally due to existing GSP treatment—institutionalized in the association agreements—not because of the short-term impact of the agreements themselves.

Slow ratification of the agreements has dampened the initial enthusiasm and the importance originally attached to them by Central and Eastern European policymakers and the public. The delay is particularly striking considering the relatively short period required to negotiate the bilateral agreements. However, as long as the documents are not in force, no progress can be made in nontrade areas such as services, capital flows, and labor migration. The outlook for cooperation in these areas remains rather mixed, with better prospects for cooperation on services and non-discrimination for capital flows (which is already established), but very limited progress on labor issues.

Despite these obstacles, quantitative analysis reveals some important trends. First, although Central and Eastern European countries have clearly benefited from improved access to the EC market, EC exports to the transforming economies grew even more rapidly than EC imports from the region. EC exports to Central and Eastern Europe increased by 71 percent between 1989 and 1992, while EC imports from Central and Eastern Europe increased by 53 percent over the same period. With the exception of Hungary, EC exports to the associated countries and to the former Soviet Union increased more rapidly than OECD exports to the same countries. In other words, trade trends ignored the asymmetric provisions of the association agreements.

Second, and corresponding to the first point, the EC trade balance with Central and Eastern Europe has improved substantially. The Community registered trade deficits with the CMEA (excluding the Soviet Union) throughout most of the 1980s. The trade deficit amounted to $0.8 billion in 1989 and to almost $1.7 billion in 1990. Yet in 1991, the EC trade balance showed a surplus of about $1.4 billion, mainly due to a large bilateral surplus with Poland. In 1992, the Community registered a trade surplus of roughly $3.3 billion, showing surpluses with all Central and Eastern European economies (table 3). In sum, the advantages of asymmetric treatment the Community granted to Central and Eastern European exports could not keep pace with the EC export offensive to the transforming economies.

Third, disaggregated statistical analysis shows a rather striking result: the dynamic growth of Central and Eastern European exports to the Community were predominantly, if not exclusively, due to export successes in the German market. Between 1989 and 1992, Central and Eastern European exports to Germany more than doubled, while exports to other EC countries experienced considerably slower growth of just 19 percent.[5]

---

5. German trade figures for 1991 and 1992 may be somewhat skewed, since they include trade with former East Germany. However, trade with East Germany shrunk dramatically after 1989; it represented less than 10 percent of its earlier value for Romania and Bulgaria, 15 percent for Hungary, and about 50 percent for Poland and Czechoslovakia. In addition, trade with West Germany was much more important than trade with East Germany well before the end of the 1980s.

Table 3   European Community: trade balances with Central and Eastern Europe, 1989–92[a] (millions of dollars)

EC balance with:	1989	1990	1991	1992
Central and Eastern Europe	–3,249	–7,339	–1,850	–1,380
Central and Eastern Europe, excluding former USSR	–835	–1,696	1,421	3,302
Former USSR[b]	–2,414	–5,643	–3,271	–4,692
Poland	–1	–1,092	1,985	1,440
Czechoslovakia	–246	–116	–350	972
Hungary	393	–157	–285	48
Romania	–2,010	–426	–195	576
Bulgaria	1,015	383	267	276

a. Data for 1989–90 include the old Federal Republic of Germany; data for 1991–92 include the unified Germany.

b. Data for 1992 include the Baltic states.

Source: Author's calculations based on *OECD Monthly Statistics of Foreign Trade*, Series A, Paris (January 1992 and August 1993).

Over the same period, German imports from Central and Eastern Europe grew at a much faster rate than its total imports; but the rest of the European Community experienced significantly lower growth in imports from Central and Eastern Europe than in total imports (table 1). Two key messages can be read from the statistical evidence:

■ The export performance of Central and Eastern Europe was mainly driven by the unique German import boom due to its reunification and only partially by improved access to the EC market.

■ Better market access conditions did not lead to a significant increase in exports to the European Community (excluding Germany).

Hence, with some exaggeration, the association agreements could be characterized as bilateral treaties with Germany and, to a lesser extent, with Italy. In fact, Germany's share in Central and Eastern European trade with the Community has substantially increased (table 4). Between 1989 and 1992, Germany's share in total EC exports remained constant at about 30 percent. However, Germany's share in EC exports to Central and Eastern Europe remained at a high level or even expanded. In 1992, Germany accounted for almost two-thirds of EC exports to Czechoslovakia and more than 50 percent of EC exports to Hungary, Poland, and the former Soviet Union.

EC import figures reveal similarly high German shares, but there is one crucial difference that underscores the impact of German unifica-

Table 4 Germany: share in EC trade with Central and Eastern Europe, 1989–92 (percentages)

	1989	1990	1991	1992
EC exports to:				
World	30.0	29.3	29.3	29.6
Central and Eastern Europe	49.0	49.5	57.6	52.6
Former USSR[a]	44.2	45.9	61.5	53.4
Poland	54.8	51.8	52.4	50.1
Czechoslovakia	55.7	58.0	63.3	65.4
Hungary	58.7	56.7	58.8	57.2
Romania	41.1	43.7	45.0	35.6
Bulgaria	47.7	42.1	40.2	38.8
EC imports from:				
World	23.0	24.1	26.7	26.9
Central and Eastern Europe	33.6	36.8	46.6	48.3
Former USSR[a]	27.1	28.3	39.2	39.7
Poland	43.6	48.0	56.2	58.4
Czechoslovakia	46.5	49.2	60.6	65.4
Hungary	49.1	52.7	55.9	57.0
Romania	28.9	34.5	40.1	44.2
Bulgaria	29.2	32.7	34.4	33.5

a. Including the Baltic states for 1992.

Source: Author's calculations based on *OECD Monthly Statistics of Foreign Trade*, Series A, Paris (January 1992 and August 1993).

tion. Germany's share in total EC imports increased by about 4 percent, from 23 percent in 1989 to almost 27 percent in 1992. However, the German share in EC imports from Central and Eastern Europe showed a far bigger increase: between 1989 and 1992, the German share in EC imports from Central and Eastern Europe rose by an average of almost 15 percentage points, ranging from an increase of 4 percentage points for Bulgaria to 19 percentage points for Czechoslovakia.

There is another important factor that contributed to the increased importance of the German market: the difference between the commodity composition of German imports and the commodity composition of imports of most other EC economies. In 1991, the German market accounted for 48 percent of all EC imports from Central and Eastern Europe; however, it absorbed more than 60 percent of EC imports of industrial consumer goods from Central and Eastern Europe

Table 5 Germany: share in EC imports from Central and Eastern Europe by commodity group, 1991

SITC group	Central and Eastern Europe	Visegrád countries
All commodities	47.5	57.8
Food and live animals	44.0	46.7
Meat	47.7	48.8
Vegetables and fruits	61.8	62.4
Raw materials	32.8	46.0
Mineral fuels	47.1	63.0
Chemicals	35.0	43.2
Organic chemicals		33.7
Medicines	48.3	50.7
Fertilizers	26.8	49.8
Explosives	47.1	48.6
Manufactured goods	51.8	61.2
Textiles	50.3	54.1
Iron and steel	50.9	54.9
Manufactures of metal	64.5	67.7
Machinery and transportation equipment	59.3	63.5
Power generators	56.6	61.3
Specialized machinery	68.8	70.1
Metalworking machinery	52.3	54.7
Electrical machinery	56.3	61.9
Automobiles	55.4	62.3
Other manufactured goods	63.1	66.3
Sanitary, plumbing, etc.	69.2	73.3
Furniture	69.1	76.4
Luggage and handbags	55.2	60.5
Apparel	63.9	66.1
Footwear	60.1	61.8

Source: Author's calculations based on OECD Trade by Commodities, Series C, Paris, 1991.

and almost 60 percent of EC machinery imports from the region (tables 5 and 6).

Fourth, the OECD countries in general, and the EC member states in particular, shifted their export priorities within the Central and Eastern European region from the former Soviet Union to the more developed and rapidly transforming Central European countries: Poland, Hungary,

Table 6 EC and Germany: imports from Central and Eastern Europe by commodity, 1989 and 1991 (percentage of total imports)

SITC group	EC imports		German imports		EC imports excluding Germany	
	1989	1991	1989	1991	1989	1991
Central and Eastern European exports						
Food and live animals	7.4	7.4	8.1	6.9	7.1	7.9
Raw materials	10.3	7.5	7.4	5.2	11.7	9.6
Mineral fuels	38.1	34.1	31.1	33.8	41.6	34.4
Chemicals	6.2	6.6	6.2	4.9	6.2	8.2
Manufactured goods	17.9	18.4	23.0	20.1	15.3	16.9
Machinery and transportation equipment	6.9	9.5	6.2	11.9	7.2	7.4
Other manufactures	9.1	11.7	14.9	15.5	6.3	8.2
Visegrád country exports						
Food and live animals	18.1	14.5	15.2	11.7	20.7	18.3
Raw materials	10.7	7.7	8.6	6.1	12.5	9.9
Mineral fuels	8.1	6.0	9.3	6.6	7.1	5.3
Chemicals	9.0	9.8	7.1	7.3	10.6	13.2
Manufactured goods	23.5	24.5	26.8	26.0	20.6	22.6
Machinery and transportation equipment	12.7	15.4	9.9	16.9	15.1	13.3
Other manufactures	15.9	20.3	20.3	23.3	12.0	16.2

Source: Author's calculations based on *OECD Trade by Commodities*, Series C, Paris, 1991.

and Czechoslovakia (the Visegrád 3). OECD countries realized that opening the more developed Central European economies provided better opportunities than opening the Balkan countries, let alone the former Soviet Union.[6] In 1989, more than half of EC exports to Central and Eastern Europe still went to the Soviet Union and only 39 percent to the Visegrád 3. By 1992, this ratio had made a 180-degree turnaround: 38 percent of all EC exports to Central and Eastern Europe went to the former Soviet Union while 54 percent went to the Visegrád countries.

---

6. In this context, it is hard to understand why the OECD countries persist in trying to convince the Visegrád countries to orient themselves eastward.

Table 7 Central and Eastern Europe: trade with the OECD and selected OECD regions and countries, 1989 and 1992
(percentage of total trade)

	Exports to:			Imports from:		
	former USSR[a]	Visegrád 3	Other[b]	former USSR[a]	Visegrád 3	Other[b]
OECD						
1989	61.4	30.8	7.8	57.1	32.5	10.4
1992	41.5	50.6	7.9	49.2	44.3	6.5
EC						
1989	52.3	38.7	9.0	55.3	33.4	11.3
1992	38.1	53.5	8.4	47.3	46.3	6.4
EFTA						
1989	61.3	33.1	5.6	59.9	36.7	3.4
1992	29.5	65.1	5.4	46.8	50.1	3.1
France						
1989	59.7	30.4	9.9	62.8	24.3	12.9
1992	44.4	39.0	16.6	64.7	28.0	7.3
Germany						
1989	47.2	44.4	8.4	44.6	45.7	9.7
1992	37.1	57.0	5.9	39.6	57.8	5.3
Italy						
1989	64.0	27.0	9.0	59.7	23.3	17.0
1992	47.0	42.0	11.0	57.5	34.8	7.7
United Kingdom						
1989	54.4	35.6	10.0	52.8	37.6	9.6
1992	30.1	62.0	7.9	50.3	42.3	7.4
Austria						
1989	34.8	57.4	7.8	29.6	65.6	4.8
1992	17.1	77.4	5.5	22.5	73.1	4.4

a. Includes the Baltic states for 1992.

b. Romania and Bulgaria.

Source: Author's calculations based on *OECD Monthly Statistics of Foreign Trade*, Series A, Paris (January 1992 and August 1993).

Interestingly, France and Italy, the more protectionist EC countries, lagged considerably in making this switch compared with Germany and the United Kingdom, the more open economies. As of 1992, the former Soviet Union remained the main export market in Central and Eastern Europe for France and Italy, despite the declining overall Soviet share of EC exports to the region. But the United Kingdom was exporting twice as much to the Visegrád group as to the former Soviet Union, and German exports to the Visegrád countries were more than 50 percent higher than German exports to the former Soviet Union (table 7).

Even more telling are the differences between EC countries in their respective imports from the Central and Eastern European countries. Although the trend is visibly toward more imports from the Visegrád countries, as of 1992 the European Community still imported more from the former Soviet Union than from the three Central European countries. Germany was the only EC country to import more from Central Europe than from the former Soviet Union (58 percent and 40 percent, respectively). The other three major EC economies (especially Italy) imported more from the former Soviet Union than from the Visegrád group. These figures could indirectly reflect access barriers that developed Central European countries faced when exporting to certain EC countries.

1993: End of the Success Story?

Recently, economic relations between the European Community and the associated countries have entered into a third, qualitatively different, and more strained stage. In the first period, from 1989 to 1991, bilateral relations developed rapidly compared with the decade-long stalemate preceding the overwhelming changes in Central and Eastern Europe. The second period, from 1991 to 1992, was characterized by an understandable slowdown, but the opportunities and policy instruments created after 1989 continued to widen cooperation. However, in the third period, starting in 1993, the widening process failed to gain momentum once the association agreements were signed. In fact, a number of adverse implications surfaced. The positive trends—which were created in the first phase—gradually weakened, or were even extinguished, by new problems.

The Central and Eastern European development process of the last few years has been threatened by two basic factors: increasing EC barriers to imports from Central and Eastern Europe and a rapidly growing trade deficit with the European Community.

Exports to the Community started to weaken in the second half of 1992. Growth rates—which had previously been outstanding—declined from month to month, although the overall economic performance remained satisfactory until the end of 1992. In 1993, Hungary and Poland experienced sharp drops in their economic performance, while the previously high Czech and Slovak export growth rates came to a near halt.[7]

---

7. Due to the introduction of new statistical methods with the implementation of the internal market, the European Union has published no monthly figures for 1993. Sporadic information is based on national statistics, raising a variety of doubts as to its reliability.

First and foremost, this decline can be explained by the prolonged EC recession. However, this is not a complete explanation because exports to the Community fell much faster than the recession and the subsequent fall in overall EC import demand would justify.

Three additional reasons deserve mention. First—and underscoring the decisive impact of the German import boom on the previous export successes of Central and Eastern Europe—Germany is going through a particularly deep recession.

Second, most of the positive effects generated by GSP treatment and the trade sections of the association agreements had a one-shot character. Central and Eastern European countries were able to boost their exports in the first years, particularly if they had export capacity on hand and the main impediment to enter EC markets was high tariffs. However, once the new room for trade expansion had been used up, no additional impact could be expected from this package.

Third, fundamental domestic developments bear most of the blame for the interruption of the success story. Over the course of the last few years, all transforming economies opted to carry out strict anti-inflationary monetary policies. This caused not only a decline in domestic production but also a sharp reduction in investment activity. As a result, little new export capacity was created; instead, Central and Eastern European exports to the European Community continued to draw on the production structure inherited from the former CMEA, which was now reoriented toward exporting to the West.

In a number of cases, this reorientation did not improve the profitability of Central and Eastern European companies. On the contrary, it gradually undermined the financial viability of many enterprises, deprived firms of investment funds, and ultimately forced them to start eating into their assets. This negative trend was aggravated by erroneous economic policy measures—such as ill-advised (or precipitate, unconsidered) implementation of bankruptcy laws and the poor timing of social welfare reforms.

In contrast to the weakening of exports to the Community, Central and Eastern European imports did not decline. EC firms seized the opportunity created by more open markets to the East and the weakened position of Central and Eastern European firms to expand their exports. Recession in the EC market was an additional driving force. The result was a rapidly growing Central and Eastern European bilateral trade deficit. Although this change was already clear in 1992, the deficit became much worse in 1993. During the first seven months of 1993, the Hungarian trade balance with the Community deteriorated by more than $1 billion and showed a deficit of about $0.7 billion, compared with a trade surplus of $0.3 billion in the same period of 1992. Despite the devaluation of the Polish zloty, Poland's trade deficit with the Community reached $1 billion by the end of August 1993. Likewise, the Czech trade balance with the Community also turned into a deficit: about $300 million in the first half of 1993, after a surplus in the same period of 1992.

There is an additional reason for concern: the Community recently started to register surpluses in its bilateral trade in certain sensitive goods. According to conventional wisdom, sensitive goods should be among the most important net surplus items of the transforming economies. But in areas such as agriculture, the EC trade deficit with Central and Eastern Europe is rapidly shrinking as a result of sharply declining imports and skyrocketing exports. This development not only contradicts the widespread expectation that the association agreements would improve Central and Eastern European trade balances with the Community, but it also contrasts with the total EC trade deficit, on a global basis, of $90 billion in 1992.

Deficiencies inherent in the association agreements aggravate the situation, especially in Central Europe, where the gap between expectations and reality has been sharp. First, the delayed ratification of significant chapters in the agreements has caused growing disappointment and even mistrust. The view is spreading that Central and Eastern Europe may have lost its priority position on the agenda of the newly renamed European Union.

Second, a sentiment toward increased protectionism has already led to some EU restrictions on exports from Central and Eastern Europe.[8] Because of the current recession in the European Union—probably representing a 1 to 2 percent decline in GDP—the view seems to prevail that some degree of protection cannot be avoided. However, this argument is extremely hard to swallow in Central and Eastern Europe, where import restrictions were liberalized despite three years of aggregate output decline cumulating to 18 to 25 percent. It is a "parody of reality" (de Vries 1993) to attribute the unhappy state of some EU firms and industries to exports from the transforming economies, inasmuch as they account for a negligible portion of total EU consumption.[9]

Third, trade in agriculture has become a stumbling block. All associ-

---

8. Imports of competitive steel products were restricted shortly after negotiations on the association agreements had been concluded. Also, the annual increases in new steel quotas are based on 1991 exports—a year with particularly low exports—not on the boom year of 1992 (Dyker 1993). Central and Eastern European politicians and economic experts wonder why their countries must suffer the consequences of the homegrown problems of the EC steel industry.

9. According to 1991 figures, EC imports of fertilizers from Central and Eastern Europe accounted for 12.5 percent of total EC fertilizer imports, while the corresponding share of fuels amounted to 11 percent. Other numbers are furniture, 6 percent; minerals and raw materials, 4.5 percent; and clothing, 4.2 percent. For all other two-digit SITC commodity groups, the portion of EC imports from Central and Eastern European countries was less than 4 percent (table 2). EC imports from Central and Eastern Europe as a percentage of total EC domestic consumption are naturally much lower.

ated countries are major agricultural exporters to the European Union; Poland and Hungary register substantial surpluses in their agricultural trade with the Union. However, over the last few years, the Central and Eastern European share in total EC imports exceeded the Central and Eastern European share in EC imports of agricultural goods (in 1991, 2.8 percent and 2.3 percent, respectively). This underrepresentation of agricultural goods is highlighted by the case of Hungary. While about half of all Hungarian exports go the European Union, only 40 percent of Hungary's agricultural exports are sold in the EU market. In addition, traditional agricultural countries in Central and Eastern Europe have been invaded by a wide range of EU agricultural goods, which threaten to kill domestic production. The competition is not based on cost and quality, but rather on subsidies, which—for obvious financial reasons—no associated country can afford.[10]

As a result, Central and Eastern European agricultural exports are stagnating while imports are skyrocketing, causing a rapid decrease in Central and Eastern European agricultural trade surpluses. In 1992, Hungarian agricultural exports to the Community increased by 1 percent, while Hungary's total agricultural exports expanded by 14 percent. Moreover, total Hungarian agricultural imports were flat, while agricultural imports from the Community expanded by more than 50 percent (Inotai 1993). This trend continued in 1993.

In the meantime, the European Union is strongly protecting the EU agricultural market and uses every opportunity to reduce external competition—through import limits, quotas based on very low initial levels of trade, and tariff reduction schemes that favor the Union.[11] A particularly harmful EU practice is the dumping of farm produce in the successor states of the Soviet Union, traditionally the most important market for the associated countries.

Fourth, restrictive EC rules of origin seriously inhibit the efficient integration of the transforming economies into the world economy. Instead of buying components from the cheapest partners, Central and Eastern European economies may be forced to buy from EU firms in order to reach the rule-of-origin thresholds stipulated in the association agree-

---

10. For example, Hungary has reduced agricultural subsidies from 30 percent in 1988 to 8 percent in 1992, while the European Union maintains a subsidization level of 45 percent. In the Czech Republic, imports of subsidized apples from the Union caused most of the domestic production to rot on the trees this autumn.

11. A large number of important agricultural products have much higher tariffs in the European Union than in the associated countries. Even an asymmetric reduction—i.e., a much steeper decline in EU tariffs than in the tariffs of the associated countries—can easily prove disadvantageous for the associated countries, because they are likely to achieve the "sensitivity margin," where further tariff cuts enable very substantial imports, much earlier than in the Union.

ments. This has already caused some trade diversion between Austria and Hungary, since Austrian components do not now count in satisfying EU rules of origin.

Finally, the associated countries were promised participation as eligible export suppliers under EC aid programs directed to Russia and other former Soviet republics. However, these promises have not been fulfilled. The economic damage is twofold. On the one hand, the expected increases in exports to Russia and other former Soviet republics have not been realized. On the other hand, Central and Eastern European exporters have been crowded out of their traditional markets for agricultural produce and certain other goods such as medicines.

Temporary Setback or Strategic Failure?

Ever since the agreements were signed, disagreements surfaced between Central and Eastern European politicians, private enterprises, and the research community regarding the evolution of the scope and nature of the agreements. Politicians missed no opportunity to emphasize the historic importance of the agreements and to praise the changing EC attitude toward the reforming countries.

Private enterprises also showed enthusiasm because they expected to gain larger market shares for their products and an influx of fresh capital and new technology. However, firms became increasingly disappointed: EC market access proved more difficult than imagined, protectionist trade barriers either remained in place or were newly applied for sensitive sectors in which Central and Eastern European firms were most competitive. Moreover, financially stronger EC competitors made a forceful appearance in the depressed Central and Eastern European markets. Most importantly, many firms felt that governments had negotiated the conditions of association without adequately taking their views or interests into account.

Although the research community never questioned the need to integrate Central and Eastern Europe into the world economy—starting with the Community because of its proximity—it never concealed its reservations about the association agreement framework. Recent developments and emerging trends seem to confirm the concerns of the research community.

The concept of the association agreements was not rooted in a well-conceived, strategic approach to the dramatic changes in the European scene. The Community has never had a well-founded *Ostpolitik*. It did not need such a strategy when the artificial division of the continent was a hard reality. In the past, the most important goal of the Community was political, not economic: it asked for diplomatic recognition in exchange for limited bilateral economic concessions. The fall of the Iron

Curtain suddenly converted the Community into a political and security anchor for the transforming countries. Quick and spectacular economic offers had to follow.

However, lacking a strategic approach, these offers—later incorporated into the framework of the association agreements—were locked within the old pattern of Community behavior. The associated countries were given a better place in the pyramid of the EC external economic network without the Community rethinking the viability of the network itself. The general view held that transformation was exclusively taking place in Central and Eastern Europe; the transforming countries would have to adjust to an unchanged and unchangeable European Community.

The Central and Eastern European countries were also largely unprepared for the new situation. Nobody had a comprehensive strategy for reshaping the patterns of a planned economy to the patterns of a market economy. The lack of a compelling approach catapulted the Community into the role of key actor. The debate over alternative forms of integration—for example, quick full membership versus delayed staged membership—became an easy substitute for a genuine strategy.

It is astonishing that no associated country prepared a detailed cost-benefit analysis of its EC association. On the contrary, economic arguments in favor of association (and full membership) were increasingly replaced by political slogans. The image of the new democratic governments was seriously damaged when economic difficulties started to surface, together with political conflicts in the domestic arena and sometimes bizarre foreign policy initiatives. No wonder that the national governments in Central and Eastern Europe considered the agreements a vitally important example of successful foreign policy and economic diplomacy.

In reality, signing an association agreement was merely a dictate of the times. The Central and Eastern European negotiators were in no position to change the Community's disposition and shape a treaty in line with the newly emerging realities of Europe. Instead, the agreements were based on well-established EC approaches, notably "organized free trade"—the centerpiece of the new pattern of relations between the Community and the transforming economies (Kramer 1993).

This approach is built on two fatally erroneous assumptions. First, it presupposes that the unprecedented challenges of transformation can be effectively met by gradual trade liberalization. Second, it assumes that the undercurrent of Western European economic malaise can be remedied by maintaining the protection of sensitive sectors.

As a consequence, trade liberalization as stipulated in the association agreements falls short. Protection has been maintained in exactly those areas where Central and Eastern Europe clearly have comparative advantage and substantial export capacity—notably agriculture, steel, textiles, and clothing. The amendments to the agreements proposed at the Copenhagen summit of June 1993 recognized the insufficient market opening, but they will not exert a major impact on economic development in the transforming countries. All the measures remain within the meticulously designed but tremendously outdated framework of orthodox EU trade policy.[12]

The main failure of the underlying agreement "philosophy" is that it tries to remedy asymmetries in the level and pattern of development that crystallized over centuries by instituting half-hearted asymmetrical trade liberalization. But it is obvious that huge GDP and GDP per capita differences cannot be overcome by trade measures alone. The aggregate GDP of the Visegrád countries is about 2 percent of that of the European Union and is still 20 percent lower than the aggregate GDP of the three least-developed EU countries—Greece, Ireland, and Portugal. The average per capita income in the Union is 8.4 times higher than that of the Visegrád countries, and that of the three least-developed EU member countries is still two to three times higher.

This development gap cannot be substantially narrowed by better access to the EU market alone. In 1992 the average market openness of the Visegrád countries (measured as exports as a share of GDP) was 23 percent, while that of the European Community was less than 21 percent. Although there is still some room to increase openness—especially in Poland—the Czech, Hungarian, and Slovak market openness figures were all well above 30 percent.

A better indicator of the development gap is the per capita export figure. In 1992 the Visegrád countries exported an average of $554 per capita (for Hungary, the top export performer, the figure was above $1,000), while the Community averaged $4,207 per capita. To narrow this huge gap, not only is further market opening required but also greater economic growth. While the first goal can be supported by trade liberalization, the second requires a number of measures going well beyond trade policy instruments.

In addition, the practical implementation of asymmetric trade concessions in favor of the associated countries raises several doubts. First, the agreements do not include asymmetric provisions in two basic areas: financial transfers and work force migration. Second, in general terms, five years of asymmetry is an extremely short period.[13] Several decades

---

12. This is illustrated by the fact that even small modifications were staunchly resisted by some EC member countries, such as the extension of rules of origin to encompass components purchased from EFTA countries, or the conversion of automatic duties into more flexible duty "ceilings."

13. Under the agreements, the European Union will implement its liberalization commitments within five years while association countries implement their commitments within ten years (box 2).

ago, the Community granted "temporary protection" to sensitive sectors such as textiles, clothing, and steel. Most of these industries have yet to become competitive. It is unreasonable to assume that the far less developed Central and Eastern European industries can become competitive in five years.

The third doubt arises from the fact that, in several cases, trade asymmetry evolved contrary to the expectations of the reforming countries. Asymmetry in agriculture often meant that imports by the associated countries reached the "sensitivity threshold" earlier than the Community expected, which triggered a mutual halt to tariff reductions. Also, different levels of agricultural subsidization created an inverse asymmetry in favor of the Community. Another surprise stems from aggressive subcontracting of clothing manufactures to Central and Eastern Europe using Western European textiles. This promoted Central and Eastern European exports of clothing to the Community, and it helped the recovery of textile factories in EC countries, but meanwhile, textile firms in the reforming countries had to be shut down because of a lack of orders.

Last but not least, doubts arise from a crucial asymmetry in nontariff protection between the Community and the transforming economies. Before 1990, the Community had already erected several highly sophisticated walls of nontariff trade protection. But rapid import liberalization in Central and Eastern Europe after 1990 was neither preceded nor accompanied by the establishment of nontariff trade barriers. As a consequence, the associated countries frequently found themselves in a disadvantageous position despite the asymmetric tariff concessions granted to them.

In sum, the research community believes that the association agreements, at least in their present form, are unable to make a significant contribution to the modernization of Central and Eastern Europe. The success of an economic and social modernization strategy relies on three international dimensions: the existence of a reliable anchor economy, substantial net financial transfers to the modernizing economies, and free market access for their exports. None of the three was taken into account when the agreement framework was shaped. However, all three are crucial for the future of the European continent.

Recent developments indicate an exhaustion of the export boom, replaced by growing trade deficits and emerging macroeconomic problems in the more advanced transforming economies. These problems signal the end of a short-lived success story. Under the present framework, it is unlikely that a return to high export growth can be achieved. Yet without high export growth, there is no room for sustained economic recovery in the transforming countries. This situation highlights the failure of the current approach.

At the end of 1993, it became obvious that the present pattern of cooperation would not generate sustained economic modernization. More generous trade liberalization, including sensitive industrial products and agricultural commodities, could have contributed to a longer export boom. Moreover, it could have narrowed the time gap between the first export wave (based on trade liberalization) and the second wave of sustainable export growth (based on structural modernization). However, this second wave will require more than trade measures.

The Central and Eastern European economies will now have to start the second and decisive wave of export-based transformation under unfavorable conditions. The "demand side" export boom has come to an end. A "supply side" approach is now required, and this will draw in imports of machinery, technology, and other inputs. As a consequence, the Central and Eastern European economies will probably experience a substantial increase in their current account deficits. Growing external indebtedness could thus become a major barrier to modernization.

Is There Hope for a New Success Story?

In the short run, the association agreements cannot be replaced with a new framework of cooperation. The nontrade chapters of the agreements have to be implemented, and the associated countries must first take advantage of opportunities they offer. But this does not mean that the transforming economies have to accept the existing agreements as the only possible model for cooperation.

The current economic and sociopolitical problems of the European Union are more than the simple expression of cyclical difficulties. The Union faces a structural and integration crisis. The structural problems are illustrated by its falling share in international export markets for manufactured goods, its high labor costs, its technological shortcomings, and the alarming rise in unemployment—currently well above 10 percent of the labor force (*The Financial Times*, 8 April 1993, 15). These problems are compounded by a crisis in the welfare state.

However, both for our topic and for the future of Europe, the deep crisis with respect to European integration holds central importance. The economic fundamentals on which the European Community was built several decades ago reflected the realities of the 1950s and 1960s, not those of the 1990s. The main constituents of this outdated model are the coal and steel community, agricultural self-sufficiency, and a customs union. Presently, these are all sources of considerable friction and conflict in the modern international economy.

Second, the political viability of the Community was built on the Franco-German alliance and on the conviction that national interests can best be represented at the Community level. The unification of Germany, the next enlargement (not only Austria, but also Sweden and Finland), the associated status of Central and Eastern Europe, and the unpredictable nature of developments in the successor states of the Soviet Union have seriously challenged this alliance, pushing the Community's center of gravity to the East. The balance between Latin and German Europe is also changing, which largely explains Southern European fears of Central and Eastern European EU membership (Franzmeyer 1993).

The need for rapid adjustment to an increasingly globalizing economy has emboldened national approaches, sparking unprecedented disagreement among member countries on the future of international trade. As a result, not only is the illusion of a "strategic Community" gone, but also the vision of a "Community of common destiny" (*Schicksalsgemeinschaft*) is seriously undermined.

Third, EU integration has lost its most important driving force: namely, a medium-term vision. Ever since the Community was established, it had a clear itinerary: from free trade and customs union to monetary and political union. When attempts to achieve its monetary and political objectives faltered, the Community tried to stimulate interest in the agenda for deepening. Maastricht was a logical element of this development. But recent developments have raised serious questions about the Maastricht plan, both in monetary and in political terms, illuminated by the breakdown of the European Monetary System and the disparate reactions to the turmoil in the former Yugoslavia.

Fourth, and most importantly, the very essence of the integration philosophy was defied by the elimination of bipolarity in Europe. The European Union, in its present form, was built to fit the requirements and challenges of a bipolar system; it was the product of ideological, military, political, and economic confrontation in Europe. But the future direction of the "European car" cannot be determined by looking through the rear-view mirror.

Central and Eastern European countries that concluded association agreements with the European Community have a fundamental feature in common. Not one of them has sufficient domestic resources to implement successful modernization strategies. The transforming countries in Central and Eastern Europe all look to the present European Union as their modernization anchor.

Beyond this shared characteristic, the transformation process has led to a increasing differentiation within the region. Yet the Community tried to push the countries into a common basket by signing virtually the same agreement with all five countries. However, it would be a mistake not to recognize the reemergence of the historical divide running across the region, splitting it into western and eastern "civilizations," to invoke Samuel Huntington's (1993) analysis. A different sequence of cooperation steps may be necessary to meet the differing needs of the two regions.

A strategic rethinking of the model for cooperation between the European Union and the transforming economies of Central and Eastern Europe should respect two basic principles:

- There can be no stability in Europe without successful economic modernization of Central and Eastern Europe.

- The new European architecture has to be designed as a framework that provides a viable European answer to the global economic challenges.

The traditional behavior of the Community toward Central and Eastern Europe is based on emergency support to the most needy countries. This approach does not offer sustainable stability because it treats the symptoms of the problem rather than its cause. Such an approach does not contribute to economic modernization because the emergency resources will generally be used to remedy the most acute social conflicts in a given national economy. Emergency support helps strengthen the rent-seeking mentality of certain actors in the transforming economies— a mentality that finds deep roots. The situation is similar at the country level. EU support can easily be diverted to those transforming economies that are the least advanced and have the least chance to become a success story, while better-endowed countries may fail in the absence of much less, but still critical, support.

Better results could be achieved through a clear-cut modernization approach based on a medium-term comprehensive package that includes substantial financial transfers from the Union to Central and Eastern Europe and an EU commitment to extend full membership to the Central and Eastern European countries in exchange for strict but reasonable conditions. The initial sum will undoubtedly be higher than the costs of one or two emergency programs. But stabilization through modernization of Central and Eastern Europe would have at least three positive impacts on the European Union: it would reduce long-term outlays, it would help redress EU economic stagnation, and, most importantly, it would improve Europe's prospects for successful global competition.

Double-digit unemployment in the Union will likely remain over the next decade. A modernization plan for Central and Eastern Europe— largely EU-financed but with contributions from others—would boost demand for imports in Central and Eastern Europe. In turn, the lion's share would be provided by Western European suppliers. Moreover, recovery in Central and Eastern Europe would create production patterns that were increasingly intertwined with those of Western Europe, especially through subcontracting networks. The resulting improvement in European competitiveness would stimulate economic activity in Western Europe and help reduce EU unemployment.

An important reason Japan, the United States, and the most advanced newly industrializing countries are gaining world market share is that their pattern of specialization based on cooperation with less-developed partners significantly cuts production costs. Correspondingly, decreasing competitiveness in the European Union reflects the Western European pattern of specialization based on cooperation among a kindred group of high-cost European countries. The modernizing Central and Eastern European countries offer a unique chance to break out of this pattern and develop mutually beneficial production networks. Central and Eastern Europe not only offer labor-cost advantages but also skill advantages, especially in engineering, chemical, and computer talent.

The half-hearted approach represented by the association agreements lacks the strategic vision and the instruments required for the foregoing scenario. To realize European prosperity requires not only a new model for European cooperation, but also a fundamental change in mentality. Instead of emphasizing the threats to Western Europe that may originate from a failure to transform the economies in Central and Eastern Europe, the positive effects of successful modernization should be stressed, both in strategic policymaking and in shaping Western European public opinion.

References

Dyker, David A. 1993. "Free Trade and Fair Trade with Eastern Europe." *RFE/RL Research Report* 2, no. 26 (25 June): 39–42.

Franzmeyer, Fritz. 1993. "Wer erhaelt Zutritt zu einer EG á la Maastricht?" *Wirtschaftsdienst* 73, no. 5: 252–57.

Handl, Vladimir. 1993. "Germany and Central Europe: 'Mitteleuropa' Restored?" *Perspectives*, no. 1: 45–51.

Huntington, Samuel. 1993. "The Clash of Civilizations?" *Foreign Affairs* 72, no. 3 (Summer).

Inotai, András. 1993. *The Economic Impacts of the Association Agreement: The Case of Hungary*. Budapest: Institute for World Economics, Budapest (April).

Kramer, Heinz. 1993. "The European Community's Response to the 'New Eastern Europe.'" *Journal of Common Market Studies* 31, no. 2 (June): 213–44.

Richter, Sándor. 1993. *East-West Trade Under Growing Western Protectionism*. Wien: Wiener Institut für Internationale Wirtschaftsvergleiche (June).

Stankovsky, Jan. 1993. "OECD-Handel mit Ost-Mitteleuropa kraeftig gewachsen." *WIFO-Monatsberichte*, no. 9: 353–61.

de Vries, Gijs M. 1993. "Hungary and the European Community—a West European View." *The World Today* 49, no. 7 (July): 139–41.

Comment

DANIEL GROS

At the outset I wish to underline how refreshing and useful it is to have, for once, a view from "East" of the European Union, which is certainly more relevant in these matters than the view from within. The term East should of course not be taken seriously since this region is very much in the center of Europe.

Given the profound changes that are taking place in that part of Europe, it is understandable that the author concentrates on the current situation. He is right in drawing attention to the fact that a 1 percent annual decline in GDP for the Union is considered to create such large social problems that protectionism may become virulent, whereas countries in Central and Eastern Europe have experienced output declines of 20 percent or more yet continue to liberalize.

However, even in the face of profound structural difficulties, one should not concentrate too much on the present but raise one's view to the long run. It is the long-run perspective that is missing in the chapter. In his introduction, Professor Inotai talks about three roles the Community has been expected to play in Central and Eastern Europe: as trade anchor, security anchor, and modernization anchor. Most of the paper dwells on the issue of trade, and the author then turns in the final sections to modernization. I will comment on the modernization aspect after I discuss trade.

Daniel Gros is Senior Research Fellow at the Centre for European Policy Studies in Brussels.

Trade

The author focuses on the question of the impact of the association agreements. Briefly, one has to admit that it is too early to tell. Before the agreements came into force, an export boom took place. Since they entered into force, there has been a break in the data collection system; while the data are not entirely reliable, it seems almost certain that the boom is over. Could one therefore argue that the agreements had a negative impact on trade? This would of course be ludicrous. The fall in the growth rates of trade—especially exports—can be explained quite easily.

First of all, these countries are experiencing considerable capital inflows—in the form of foreign direct investment and official capital or grants—which necessarily have a current-account deficit as their counterpart. Real exchange rates thus appreciated, and export growth declined. Portugal and Spain experienced something similar upon joining the Community. If you add the adverse impact on import demand of the current recession in Western Europe and the general proposition that trade liberalization, even if asymmetrical, has little to do with the trade balance, it is not too surprising that the export boom has come to a halt, if only temporarily.

En passant, it is also useful to recall the Lerner symmetry proposition: an export tax is equivalent to an import tax. This powerful proposition is too often forgotten. It implies that an import tax limits both exports and imports. Somebody has expressed this by saying a tax on trade is a tax on trade. Thus, the remaining import restrictions of the European Union limit not only EU imports, but also EU exports.

The trade part of the agreements is certainly not perfect. But can one hold the imperfections responsible for slow growth of exports? There is absolutely no evidence for this view at the microeconomic level. There have been one or two cases of trade barriers in the steel sector, but they are no worse than the regulations governing EU trade in agricultural products with the rest of the world. In short, the imperfections of the agreements are deplorable but not really relevant to the difficulties experienced by the associated countries at present.

Modernization

The strategic issue that deserved more attention in the paper was a detailed and concrete policy prescription. The author's statement contains the essence of the basic idea:

> Better results could be achieved through a clear-cut modernization approach based on a medium-term comprehensive package that includes substantial

financial transfers from the Union to Central and Eastern Europe and an EU commitment to extend full membership to the Central and Eastern European countries in exchange for strict but reasonable conditions.

This medium-term comprehensive package closely resembles the Maastricht convergence program. The author summarizes the essence of the approach to convergence the Union is currently taking. However, he does not go beyond this brief statement. In particular, he fails to mention that since the Copenhagen EC Summit of July 1993 the prospect for eventual membership is clear although details are still lacking.

In my view, these details could be provided by an official convergence program jointly agreed upon by the European Union and the Visegrád countries. This convergence program would provide automatic selection, in the sense that countries that make the grade would be guaranteed membership; countries that do not perform well would not become members. This idea has been accepted by the European Union and the Visegrád governments. It would have been interesting to hear the author's view on this issue.

The crucial elements of a convergence program are its conditions and the size of required financial transfers. With regard to financial transfers, the author should have discussed the two central issues: how much will be needed, and how much can be absorbed. Brenton and Gros (1993) find that the Visegrád countries should expect at least 200 ECU annually per capita, which is equivalent to about 10 percent of GDP. If one adds the requirement that 50 percent of sponsored projects have to be cofinanced by the recipient government, it becomes clear that transfers of this magnitude are not easily absorbed. The recipient states would have to spend about 20 percent of their GDP on infrastructure and other investments financed out of the structural funds of the European Union. This is equal to the current investment-to-GDP ratios of the transforming countries. If this scenario becomes reality, investment in these countries might almost double. Moreover, the 50 percent cofinancing funds will have to be raised through taxes; this has huge budgetary implications.

Perhaps even more important is the first question concerning the conditions for membership, which are addressed at length in Gros and Ludlow (1992). A brief summary will suffice here. It is useful to distinguish three main areas of convergence:

■ **Macroeconomic**. Achieving monetary union is the ultimate goal. Although its general aim is clear—low inflation, sustainable fiscal policy—it is also apparent that considerable work on a number of fiscal issues needs to be undertaken.

■ **Microeconomic**. This area comprises the enormous set of laws and regulations that make up a market economy. To become full members of the European Union, it is obvious that the Central European countries should make sure that their legislation is compatible with that of the Union. Two slogans—approximation of laws and adoption of the *acquis communautaire*—summarize the vast legislative program that makes up this part of the convergence program.

■ **Implementation**. This is the most difficult part. If the Visegrád countries want to become credible candidates for membership, they have to implement EU laws and regulations in the same manner as member countries. This process is the essence of the modernization the author calls for.

The Treaty of Rome establishes that any European country with a democratic structure and, we would add today, a market economy can join. The associated states already have established democratic systems and are well on their way to implementing market economics. Thus, they will soon fulfill these two broad criteria. However, because they would be joining an economic and monetary union, they will also have to satisfy the convergence criteria for the European Monetary Union (EMU). It would not be necessary for them to satisfy all criteria at the time they join, but they must have the instruments that would enable them to join EMU within a reasonable period.

However, the real debate revolves around the slogan "health, not wealth." Some argue that the Union cannot afford new members whose income per capita is much lower than that of its current members. Gros and Ludlow (1992) argue that this budgetary burden would be bearable provided enough EFTA countries join at the same time.

Many discussions of the shortcomings of the association agreements focus on the contingent protectionism contained in the agreements and point out that certain sectors and regions of the European Union will undoubtedly ask for protection. This point of view neglects the fact that these dangers can be combatted if there is enough overall political support for liberalization. The trick is to generate enough public support for trade liberalization (and eventual enlargement) of the Union. In building public support, economists should be the ones to point out the potential for economic gains.

The general point that the author does not seem to take into account is that the welfare gains from trade liberalization—through first a free trade agreement, then possibly a European Economic Area, and finally EMU—arise not from higher exports, but from trade creation. The appropriate question is this: are the net welfare gains large? The answer: probably yes. But one needs to take the next step and ask, will there be any losers? The general presumption is that the EU agriculture, steel, and textiles industries will lose out. Is this true? Almost certainly not for textiles. In agriculture the situation is also not clear-cut. If one adds in the relatively high skill endowment of the Visegrád countries, it is no longer plain that they will primarily compete with the poorer regions in the European Union. Indeed, a recent study suggests the opposite; some of the poorer regions (Greece, southern Italy) will actually gain more than the richer regions. All these issues deserve careful study.

The fundamental point is that the association agreements constitute only a stepping stone toward membership. It is a slippery stone that cannot be relied upon to support the full weight of the relationship. If one only looks at these agreements, there are indeed reasons to be worried about their imperfections. However, with the prospect of full membership, which will go much beyond the agreements, the existing imperfections become irrelevant. It is up to the European Union and the associated states to work in close cooperation to ensure that the potentially protectionist elements in the association agreements cannot be used because the process of integration has gone beyond free trade alone.

References

Brenton, Paul, and Daniel Gros. 1993. *The Budgetary Implications of EC Enlargement.* Working Document No. 78. Brussels: Centre for European Policy Studies (May).

Gros, Daniel, and Peter Ludlow. 1992. *The European Union and the Future of Europe.* Brussels: Centre for European Policy Studies (October).

Comment

EGON MATZNER

While I fully agree with Professor Inotai's paper, my comments are an attempt to deepen and extend his arguments in a way that may be useful for designing political action. Inotai stresses the gap in development between the former centrally planned economies and the advanced market economies. The mere size of the "asymmetries in the level and pattern of development . . . [cannot be overcome] by instituting half-hearted asymmetrical trade liberalization." Inotai concludes that "[to] narrow this huge gap, not only is further market opening required but also greater economic growth."

However, the present course of events hardly ensures an upturn in economic growth. In the years since the end of central planning and its rocky replacement by market forces, no net investment has been achieved. This is a bad omen since the very essence of a market economy is to increase wealth. Even in areas where the transforming countries have a competitive advantage (such as agriculture), trade deficits occur. Sometimes these are accompanied by the collapse of traditional markets for domestic output, as in the case of subsidized apple imports from the European Union to Poland and the Czech Republic. In sum, association agreements so far have not been a stimulus for investment.

Inotai's study clearly indicates that a change in transformation strategy is needed. The new strategy would have to be based on two pillars (Kregel, Matzner, and Grabher 1992). The first is the creation of a domestic economic and social context that induces investment both to modernize and to expand capacity. Such a context ought to be inspired by the successful post–World War II reconstruction of Western Europe under auspices of the Organization for European Economic Cooperation (OEEC). By contrast, in the erstwhile communist countries, the socioeconomic context now induces the destruction of domestic output potential. The second pillar would be the creation of an international con-

Egon Matzner is Professor and Dean at TU-Vienna and Director of the Research Unit for Socioeconomics at the Austrian Academy of Sciences.

text that promotes the expansion of viable production capacity. Inotai's paper shows that such a context is still missing. Notable is the forecast that a pro-growth environment is not likely to emerge in the recessionary climate that prevails throughout the industrial world.

I want to draw attention to a causal factor that has long been known to destroy potential output and employment and is now hampering economic recovery in Western Europe and paralyzing economic reconstruction in Eastern Europe: asymmetric international adjustment rules (Tobin 1982; Kregel 1993). The rules of the International Monetary Fund rightly impose a restrictive economic policy on countries with large and lasting balance of payments deficits. However, they do not impose commensurate expansionary policies on the corresponding surplus countries. It is obvious that this asymmetry has a constrictive impact on effective demand and thus on potential investment and future jobs.

Asymmetric international adjustment rules have long had damaging effects. The pleas of the United States urging surplus countries such as West Germany and Japan to expand their economies have become something of a tradition. The asymmetrical rules have become even more detrimental since the end of the Bretton Woods era. They are newly built into the convergence criteria of the Maastricht Treaty, which imposes restrictive policies on member countries that violate the Maastricht norms but refrains from binding those countries that have already fulfilled the criteria to initiate expansionary measures (Bean 1992).

Given the rules of asymmetric adjustment within the IMF and the European Union, it should be no surprise that the international outlook for growth and employment is not good, despite the dire need for expansion in the advanced countries, and even more so in the transforming countries.

To summarize, what is needed is a strengthening of the two pillars in order to improve the prospects of the transforming economies in Central and Eastern Europe, as Inotai argues so convincingly. Faster growth is also essential for boosting the economic performance of the established industrial countries.

References

Bean, C. R. 1992. "Economic and Monetary Union in Europe." *Journal of Economic Perspectives* 6, no. 4: 31–52.

Kregel, J. A. 1993. "A Post-Keynesian Explanation of the Causes of the Current World Slump." Paper presented at the 11th Biannual Keynes Seminar. Canterbury: University of Kent (November).

Kregel, J. A., E. Matzner, and G. Grabher. 1992. *The Market-Shock: An Agenda for Socio-Economic Reconstruction of Central and Eastern Europe.* Ann Arbor, MI: Michigan University Press.

Tobin, J. 1982. "Adjustment Responsibilities of Surplus and Deficit Countries." In James Tobin, *Essays in Economic Theory and Policy.* Cambridge, MA: MIT Press.

Comment

RICHARD PORTES

I agree with the main propositions of this hard-hitting, strongly argued paper. Most of my comments, therefore, will go toward sharpening those propositions so as to make the argument more robust to the kind of defensive reactions one might expect and that we did indeed hear in the conference discussion.

A key theme in András Inotai's analysis is the Central and East European countries' need for a "modernization anchor," which the European Community (now the Union) should provide. Early in the transition, I stressed two possible facets of such a role for the Community (Portes 1991a, 1991b): first, to reinforce the credibility of Central and Eastern Europe's transformation programs by giving them an anti-interventionist "peg" through agreements with the Community to move rapidly to political democracy and the market economy and within the framework of a well-defined path toward ultimate EC membership and second, to give this framework operational content in the form of commitments to adopt relevant EC institutional forms, legislation, standards, and so on. Inotai rightly puts the modernization process in the historical context of Eastern Europe's political and economic development, but I should like to see a more detailed specification of the anchor.

The discussion in the paper of the development of the Community itself and its dealings with Eastern Europe since the 1950s is extremely useful. The word "crisis" is overused, and Inotai's "EC integration crisis" is no exception. But I have for some time maintained that the Commu-

---

Richard Portes is Director of the Centre for Economic Policy Research in London.

nity must deepen in order to widen successfully; Maastricht and the sequel have not in practice given us that deepening. Thus we cannot have the medium- and long-term vision that Inotai would like to see: a well-specified process for the Central and Eastern European countries' accession to the European Union. Without it, the Union will only slowly reform its long-standing habits in dealing with Eastern Europe: that is, one-on-one bargaining, with the defensive economic stance that Inotai criticizes. One symbol of this attitude is the reluctance to drop the "state trading" label that has traditionally been used to justify EC protectionist measures against the countries of Central and Eastern Europe. And even when the Community formally concedes that progress toward building a market economy has been sufficient in a specific country, one still encounters the same underlying arguments at a general level from some member states and even from some quarters in the Commission.

I have little to add to the paper's analysis of recent trade volumes and patterns. The explosive growth of Central and Eastern European exports to the West in 1990–92 does conclusively refute those who claimed these countries couldn't compete—that quality was unacceptable, marketing was poor, and so on. Inotai is probably right to stress GSP treatment in addition to the three powerful forces of price competitiveness (with depreciated exchange rates), supply-side push (responding to the fall in demand at home and throughout the region), and the German import boom. He also draws our attention to two important facts: the wide range of products participating in this export growth—not just the "sensitive" goods—and the unwelcome (to Central and Eastern Europe) and subsidized expansion of EC agricultural exports to the East.

Looking further into the future, Inotai reinforces the early judgment of a report by the Centre for Economic Policy Research (1990) that Central and Eastern Europe's comparative advantage should lie in skill-intensive goods (see also Hamilton and Winters 1992). But investment is necessary to develop these export capacities. Domestic investment has fallen sharply with the disastrous fall in output, and foreign investment has been disappointingly low. Much of the capital and associated technology must come from abroad. I do not believe that the region's competitiveness in human-capital-intensive industries will be endangered by any likely appreciation of their real exchange rates.

Any attack on the association agreements should begin by recognizing that they could have been significantly worse. Whatever their rhetoric, some member countries in practice resisted to the end any "concessions," and the mandate of the Commission's negotiators was consequently far from the open, forthcoming stance that the Community should have taken. Many of Inotai's criticisms are in my view fully justified. That said, I would suggest three important qualifications to his negative assessment.

First, the provisions for "approximation of laws" in the agreements can be viewed as part of a "transformation strategy," or modernization anchor of the kind Inotai and I see as essential. These provisions are indeed politically asymmetrical because the Central and Eastern European countries simply accepted the obligation to import EC laws and institutions without gaining any right to influence them. But the provisions do offer a rule-based framework that will tie the hands of policymakers against intervention and any retrogression to past practices.

Second, there is a contradiction between Inotai's earlier assessment of comparative advantages (see above) and his statement that in the agreements, "protection is maintained in the areas where Central and Eastern Europe has comparative advantage," where these are identified as the "sensitive" sectors of steel, textiles, and clothing. The difference between short- and medium-run opportunities for export growth should be stressed.

Finally, Inotai's criticism of the aid provided by the Community is excessive. Three criteria for such aid have been agreed on both sides: that it be cost-effective, fast-disbursing, and demand-led (responsive to the recipient country's priorities). It is very difficult to reconcile these requirements. Typically, it takes much longer for the recipients to specify their priorities than it would for the donors to impose theirs; demand-led aid is prone to exploitation by rent seekers and hence may not be cost-effective; spending fast may be conducive to waste.

In this regard, the countries of Central and Eastern Europe themselves have not been without fault, and they have made other policy mistakes as well. I believe these countries have consistently missed opportunities to act jointly, most prominently in their negotiation of the association agreements, where a united front squarely based on political imperatives might have significantly altered the framework of the discussion. Their willingness to accept passively the breakdown of intraregional trade, with only feeble efforts toward a free trade area, is another case. Inotai is quite negative—in my view, quite wrongly—on intraregional cooperation. He suspects that suggestions of this kind coming from the European Union are intended to redirect Eastern exports away from the member countries and to reduce the pressure to extend EU membership. He also claims that the European Union is imposing a common framework on both the Visegrád group and the other countries of the region, thus ignoring deep historical, cultural, and economic differences among them. This criticism might be interpreted as a Visegrád plea to let them in first.

I believe this view is unnecessarily and unproductively divisive. The extreme case is the occasional remark from the Czech Republic that it is ready for EU membership now, with the implicit or even explicit demand for special treatment, and that their neighbors are not ready. Such an approach overlooks important possibilities for cooperation that would in no way delay accession to membership (Nuti and Portes 1993). And in practice, the European Union is highly likely to deal with the Visegrád countries simultaneously when it comes to membership negotiations, just as it is now dealing jointly with the EFTA countries.

Moreover, the emphasis on national particularity obscures the potentially useful lessons to be gained from the experience of other countries in the region as well as from the southern-periphery countries of the European Union: how to influence the location and character of foreign investment, how to ensure that aid goes effectively to infrastructure and the creation of appropriate incentives rather than to rent seeking, and how to design fiscal reforms, financial restructuring, and central bank independence. Why should any country think it is so special that it cannot learn from the experience of countries that are less as well as more developed than itself? Cooperation need not impose a common model in order to promote this learning.

I conclude with a few observations on EU policies. First, we should already be thinking in terms of the continental market, not just the EU market. Thus, a restructuring policy for the steel industry that does not explicitly include the countries of Central and Eastern Europe from the outset makes little long-run sense (Brittan 1994). Second, the European Union should indeed be more generous with aid; the current Poland and Hungary Assistance for Economic Restructuring (PHARE) program budget is only a tenth of what these countries would get if they were in the Union and thus were recipients of structural funds and transfers through the Common Agricultural Policy (Baldwin et al. 1992). Partly because of the lack of such funds, even the Visegrád countries cannot expect membership within this decade.

Nevertheless, there should be continued pressure on the Union to strengthen its commitment, to define more precisely the path to membership, and meanwhile to liberalize trade access further and avoid using measures of contingent protection. I think Inotai underestimates the advance made at the Copenhagen European Council in June 1993, but progress must not slacken. To talk of convergence programs for Central and Eastern Europe seems to me misleading, however: the Union is not about to promise membership upon the attainment of specific convergence conditions, so the analogy to the Maastricht provisions for EMU is misplaced. It is likely that significant progress along these lines does require deepening of the existing Union. Pan-European structural policies are not feasible without greater willingness among member countries to take a pan-European view and to incorporate that in EU decision making. A substantial increase in aid and openness to Central and Eastern Europe is not likely unless the European Union does develop the basis for a common foreign policy. All this will take time, but there is no reason why the countries of Central and Eastern Europe should be passive while being patient.

References

Baldwin, Richard, et al. 1992. *Is Bigger Better? The Economics of EC Enlargement.* CEPR Special Report No. 3. London: Center for Economic Policy Research.

Brittan, L. 1994. *The Future of the European Economy.* London: Centre for Economic Policy Research.

Centre for Economic Policy Research (CEPR). 1990. *Monitoring European Integration 1: The Impact of Eastern Europe.* London.

Hamilton, C., and L. A. Winters. 1992 "Opening up international trade with Eastern Europe." *Economic Policy* 14: 77–116.

Nuti, M., and R. Portes. 1993. "Central Europe: the Way Forward." In R. Portes, *Economic Transformation in Central Europe.* London: Centre for Economic Policy Research.

Portes, R. 1991a. "The European Community and Eastern Europe after 1992." In T. Padoa-Schioppa, *Europe after 1992: Three Essays.* Princeton Essay in International Finance No. 182.

Portes, R. 1991b. "The Path of Reform in Central and Eastern Europe: an Introduction." *European Economy,* Special Edition No. 2: 1–15.

Other Publications from the
Institute for International Economics

POLICY ANALYSES IN INTERNATIONAL ECONOMICS Series

1   **The Lending Policies of the International Monetary Fund**
John Williamson/*August 1982*
ISBN paper 0-88132-000-5   72 pp.

2   **"Reciprocity": A New Approach to World Trade Policy?**
William R. Cline/*September 1982*
ISBN paper 0-88132-001-3   41 pp.

3   **Trade Policy in the 1980s**
C. Fred Bergsten and William R. Cline/*November 1982*
(out of print)   ISBN paper 0-88132-002-1   84 pp.
Partially reproduced in the book *Trade Policy in the 1980s.*

4   **International Debt and the Stability of the World Economy**
William R. Cline/*September 1983*
ISBN paper 0-88132-010-2   134 pp.

5   **The Exchange Rate System, Second Edition**
John Williamson/*September 1983, rev. June 1985*
(out of print)   ISBN paper 0-88132-034-X   61 pp.

6   **Economic Sanctions in Support of Foreign Policy Goals**
Gary Clyde Hufbauer and Jeffrey J. Schott/*October 1983*
ISBN paper 0-88132-014-5   109 pp.

7   **A New SDR Allocation?**
John Williamson/*March 1984*
ISBN paper 0-88132-028-5   61 pp.

8   **An International Standard for Monetary Stabilization**
Ronald I. McKinnon/*March 1984*
ISBN paper 0-88132-018-8   108 pp.

9   **The Yen/Dollar Agreement: Liberalizing Japanese Capital Markets**
Jeffrey A. Frankel/*December 1984*
ISBN paper 0-88132-035-8   86 pp.

10 **Bank Lending to Developing Countries: The Policy Alternatives**
C. Fred Bergsten, William R. Cline, and John Williamson/*April 1985*
ISBN paper 0-88132-032-3   221 pp.

11 **Trading for Growth: The Next Round of Trade Negotiations**
Gary Clyde Hufbauer and Jeffrey J. Schott/*September 1985*
ISBN paper 0-88132-033-1   109 pp.

12 **Financial Intermediation Beyond the Debt Crisis**
Donald R. Lessard and John Williamson/*September 1985*
ISBN paper 0-88132-021-8   130 pp.

13 **The United States-Japan Economic Problem**
C. Fred Bergsten and William R. Cline/*October 1985, 2d ed. January 1987*
(out of print)   ISBN paper 0-88132-060-9   180 pp.

14 **Deficits and the Dollar: The World Economy at Risk**
Stephen Marris/*December 1985, 2d ed. November 1987*
ISBN paper 0-88132-067-6   415 pp.

15 **Trade Policy for Troubled Industries**
Gary Clyde Hufbauer and Howard F. Rosen/*March 1986*
ISBN paper 0-88132-020-X   111 pp.

16 **The United States and Canada: The Quest for Free Trade**
Paul Wonnacott, with an Appendix by John Williamson/*March 1987*
ISBN paper 0-88132-056-0   188 pp.

17 **Adjusting to Success: Balance of Payments Policy
in the East Asian NICs**
Bela Balassa and John Williamson/*June 1987, rev. April 1990*
ISBN paper 0-88132-101-X   160 pp.

18 **Mobilizing Bank Lending to Debtor Countries**
William R. Cline/*June 1987*
ISBN paper 0-88132-062-5   100 pp.

19 **Auction Quotas and United States Trade Policy**
C. Fred Bergsten, Kimberly Ann Elliott, Jeffrey J. Schott,
and Wendy E. Takacs/*September 1987*
ISBN paper 0-88132-050-1   254 pp.

20 **Agriculture and the GATT: Rewriting the Rules**
Dale E. Hathaway/*September 1987*
ISBN paper 0-88132-052-8   169 pp.

21 **Anti-Protection: Changing Forces in United States Trade Politics**
I. M. Destler and John S. Odell/*September 1987*
ISBN paper 0-88132-043-9   220 pp.

22 **Targets and Indicators: A Blueprint for the International
Coordination of Economic Policy**
John Williamson and Marcus H. Miller/*September 1987*
ISBN paper 0-88132-051-X   118 pp.

23 **Capital Flight: The Problem and Policy Responses**
Donald R. Lessard and John Williamson/*December 1987*
ISBN paper 0-88132-059-5   80 pp.

24 **United States-Canada Free Trade: An Evaluation of the Agreement**
Jeffrey J. Schott/*April 1988*
ISBN paper 0-88132-072-2   48 pp.

25 **Voluntary Approaches to Debt Relief**
John Williamson/*September 1988, rev. May 1989*
ISBN paper 0-88132-098-6   80 pp.

26 **American Trade Adjustment: The Global Impact**
William R. Cline/*March 1989*
ISBN paper 0-88132-095-1   98 pp.

27 **More Free Trade Areas?**
Jeffrey J. Schott/*May 1989*
ISBN paper 0-88132-085-4   88 pp.

28 **The Progress of Policy Reform in Latin America**
John Williamson/*January 1990*
ISBN paper 0-88132-100-1   106 pp.

29 The Global Trade Negotiations: What Can Be Achieved?
Jeffrey J. Schott/*September 1990*
ISBN paper 0-88132-137-0   72 pp.

30 Economic Policy Coordination: Requiem or Prologue?
Wendy Dobson/*April 1991*
ISBN paper 0-88132-102-8   162 pp.

31 The Economic Opening of Eastern Europe
John Williamson/*May 1991*
ISBN paper 0-88132-186-9   92 pp.

32 Eastern Europe and the Soviet Union in the World Economy
Susan M. Collins and Dani Rodrik/*May 1991*
ISBN paper 0-88132-157-5   152 pp.

33 African Economic Reform: The External Dimension
Carol Lancaster/*June 1991*
ISBN paper 0-88132-096-X   82 pp.

34 Has the Adjustment Process Worked?
Paul R. Krugman/*October 1991*
ISBN paper 0-88132-116-8   80 pp.

35 From Soviet disUnion to Eastern Economic Community?
Oleh Havrylyshyn and John Williamson/*October 1991*
ISBN paper 0-88132-192-3   84 pp.

36 Global Warming: The Economic Stakes
William R. Cline/*May 1992*
ISBN paper 0-88132-172-9   128 pp.

37 Trade and Payments After Soviet Disintegration
John Williamson/*June 1992*
ISBN paper 0-88132-173-7   96 pp.

38 Trade and Migration: NAFTA and Agriculture
Philip L. Martin/*October 1993*
ISBN paper 0-88132-201-6   160 pp.

BOOKS

IMF Conditionality
John Williamson, editor/*1983*
ISBN cloth 0-88132-006-4   695 pp.

Trade Policy in the 1980s
William R. Cline, editor/*1983*
ISBN cloth 0-88132-008-1   810 pp.
ISBN paper 0-88132-031-5   810 pp.

Subsidies in International Trade
Gary Clyde Hufbauer and Joanna Shelton Erb/*1984*
ISBN cloth 0-88132-004-8   299 pp.

International Debt: Systemic Risk and Policy Response
William R. Cline/*1984*
ISBN cloth 0-88132-015-3   336 pp.

Trade Protection in the United States: 31 Case Studies
Gary Clyde Hufbauer, Diane E. Berliner, and Kimberly Ann Elliott/*1986*
ISBN paper 0-88132-040-4   371 pp.

Toward Renewed Economic Growth in Latin America
Bela Balassa, Gerardo M. Bueno, Pedro-Pablo Kuczynski,
and Mario Henrique Simonsen/*1986*
(out of stock)   ISBN paper 0-88132-045-5   205 pp.

Capital Flight and Third World Debt
Donald R. Lessard and John Williamson, editors/*1987*
(out of print)   ISBN paper 0-88132-053-6   270 pp.

The Canada-United States Free Trade Agreement:
The Global Impact
Jeffrey J. Schott and Murray G. Smith, editors/*1988*
ISBN paper 0-88132-073-0   211 pp.

World Agricultural Trade: Building a Consensus
William M. Miner and Dale E. Hathaway, editors/*1988*
ISBN paper 0-88132-071-3   226 pp.

Japan in the World Economy
Bela Balassa and Marcus Noland/*1988*
ISBN paper 0-88132-041-2   306 pp.

America in the World Economy: A Strategy for the 1990s
C. Fred Bergsten/*1988*
ISBN cloth 0-88132-089-7   235 pp.
ISBN paper 0-88132-082-X   235 pp.

Managing the Dollar: From the Plaza to the Louvre
Yoichi Funabashi/*1988, 2d ed. 1989*
ISBN paper 0-88132-097-8   307 pp.

United States External Adjustment and the World Economy
William R. Cline/*May 1989*
ISBN paper 0-88132-048-X   392 pp.

Free Trade Areas and U.S. Trade Policy
Jeffrey J. Schott, editor/*May 1989*
ISBN paper 0-88132-094-3   400 pp.

Dollar Politics: Exchange Rate Policymaking in the United States
I. M. Destler and C. Randall Henning/*September 1989*
ISBN paper 0-88132-079-X   192 pp.

Latin American Adjustment: How Much Has Happened?
John Williamson, editor/*April 1990*
ISBN paper 0-88132-125-7   480 pp.

The Future of World Trade in Textiles and Apparel
William R. Cline/*1987, 2d ed. June 1990*
ISBN paper 0-88132-110-9   344 pp.

Completing the Uruguay Round: A Results-Oriented Approach
to the GATT Trade Negotiations
Jeffrey J. Schott, editor/*September 1990*
ISBN paper 0-88132-130-3   256 pp.

Economic Sanctions Reconsidered (in two volumes)
Economic Sanctions Reconsidered: Supplemental Case Histories
Gary Clyde Hufbauer, Jeffrey J. Schott, and Kimberly Ann Elliott/*1985, 2d ed.*
December 1990

ISBN cloth 0-88132-115-X	928 pp.
ISBN paper 0-88132-105-2	928 pp.

Economic Sanctions Reconsidered: History and Current Policy
Gary Clyde Hufbauer, Jeffrey J. Schott, and Kimberly Ann Elliott/*December 1990*

ISBN cloth 0-88132-136-2	288 pp.
ISBN paper 0-88132-140-0	288 pp.

Pacific Basin Developing Countries: Prospects for the Future
Marcus Noland/*January 1991*

ISBN cloth 0-88132-141-9	250 pp.
ISBN paper 0-88132-081-1	250 pp.

Currency Convertibility in Eastern Europe
John Williamson, editor/*October 1991*

ISBN cloth 0-88132-144-3	396 pp.
ISBN paper 0-88132-128-1	396 pp.

Foreign Direct Investment in the United States
Edward M. Graham and Paul R. Krugman/*1989, 2d ed. October 1991*

ISBN paper 0-88132-139-7	200 pp.

International Adjustment and Financing: The Lessons of 1985-1991
C. Fred Bergsten, editor/*January 1992*

ISBN paper 0-88132-112-5	336 pp.

North American Free Trade: Issues and Recommendations
Gary Clyde Hufbauer and Jeffrey J. Schott/*April 1992*

ISBN cloth 0-88132-145-1	392 pp.
ISBN paper 0-88132-120-6	392 pp.

American Trade Politics
I. M. Destler/*1986, 2d ed. June 1992*

ISBN cloth 0-88132-164-8	400 pp.
ISBN paper 0-88132-188-5	400 pp.

Narrowing the U.S. Current Account Deficit
Allen J. Lenz/*June 1992*

ISBN cloth 0-88132-148-6	640 pp.
ISBN paper 0-88132-103-6	640 pp.

The Economics of Global Warming
William R. Cline/*June 1992*

ISBN cloth 0-88132-150-8	416 pp.
ISBN paper 0-88132-132-X	416 pp.

U.S. Taxation of International Income: Blueprint for Reform
Gary Clyde Hufbauer, assisted by Joanna M. van Rooij/*October 1992*

ISBN cloth 0-88132-178-8	304 pp.
ISBN paper 0-88132-134-6	304 pp.

Who's Bashing Whom? Trade Conflict in High-Technology Industries
Laura D'Andrea Tyson/*November 1992*

ISBN cloth 0-88132-151-6	352 pp.
ISBN paper 0-88132-106-0	352 pp.

Korea in the World Economy
Il SaKong/*January 1993*

| | ISBN cloth 0-88132-184-2 | 328 pp. |
| | ISBN paper 0-88132-106-0 | 328 pp. |

Pacific Dynamism and the International Economic System
C. Fred Bergsten and Marcus Noland, editors/*May 1993*

ISBN paper 0-88132-196-6   424 pp.

Economic Consequences of Soviet Disintegration
John Williamson, editor/*May 1993*

ISBN paper 0-88132-190-7   664 pp.

Reconcilable Differences? United States-Japan Economic Conflict
C. Fred Bergsten and Marcus Noland/*June 1993*

ISBN paper 0-88132-129-X   296 pp.

Does Foreign Exchange Intervention Work?
Kathryn M. Dominguez and Jeffrey A. Frankel/*September 1993*

ISBN paper 0-88132-104-4   192 pp.

Sizing Up U.S. Export Disincentives
J. David Richardson/*September 1993*

ISBN paper 0-88132-107-9   192 pp.

NAFTA: An Assessment
Gary Clyde Hufbauer and Jeffrey J. Schott/*rev. ed. October 1993*

ISBN paper 0-88132-199-0   216 pp.

Adjusting to Volatile Energy Prices
Philip K. Verleger, Jr./*November 1993*

ISBN paper 0-88132-069-2   288 pp.

The Political Economy of Policy Reform
John Williamson, editor/*January 1994*

ISBN paper 0-88132-195-8   624 pp.

Measuring the Costs of Protection in the United States
Gary Clyde Hufbauer and Kimberly Ann Elliott/*January 1994*

ISBN paper 0-88132-108-7   144 pp.

The Dynamics of Korean Economic Development
Cho Soon/*March 1994*

ISBN paper 0-88132-162-1   272 pp.

Reviving the European Union
C. Randall Henning, Eduard Hochreiter and Gary Clyde Hufbauer/*April 1994*

ISBN paper 0-88132-208-3   192 pp.

SPECIAL REPORTS

1   **Promoting World Recovery: A Statement on Global Economic Strategy by Twenty-six Economists from Fourteen Countries**/*December 1982*
(out of print)   ISBN paper 0-88132-013-7   45 pp.

2   **Prospects for Adjustment in Argentina, Brazil, and Mexico: Responding to the Debt Crisis**
John Williamson, editor/*June 1983*
(out of print)   ISBN paper 0-88132-016-1   71 pp.

3   Inflation and Indexation: Argentina, Brazil, and Israel
    John Williamson, editor/*March 1985*
                        ISBN paper 0-88132-037-4   191 pp.

4   **Global Economic Imbalances**
    C. Fred Bergsten, editor/*March 1986*
                        ISBN cloth 0-88132-038-2   126 pp.
                        ISBN paper 0-88132-042-0   126 pp.

5   **African Debt and Financing**
    Carol Lancaster and John Williamson, editors/*May 1986*
    (out of print)   ISBN paper 0-88132-044-7   229 pp.

6   **Resolving the Global Economic Crisis: After Wall Street**
    Thirty-three Economists from Thirteen Countries/*December 1987*
                        ISBN paper 0-88132-070-6   30 pp.

7   **World Economic Problems**
    Kimberly Ann Elliott and John Williamson, editors/*April 1988*
                        ISBN paper 0-88132-055-2   298 pp.

    Reforming World Agricultural Trade
    Twenty-nine Professionals from Seventeen Countries/*1988*
                        ISBN paper 0-88132-088-9   42 pp.

8   **Economic Relations Between the United States and Korea:**
    Conflict or Cooperation?
    Thomas O. Bayard and Soo-Gil Young, editors/*January 1989*
                        ISBN paper 0-88132-068-4   192 pp.

FORTHCOMING

Reciprocity and Retaliation: An Evaluation of Tough Trade Policies
Thomas O. Bayard and Kimberly Ann Elliott

The Globalization of Industry and National Economic Policies
C. Fred Bergsten and Edward M. Graham

The New Tripolar World Economy: Toward Collective Leadership
C. Fred Bergsten and C. Randall Henning

International Debt Reexamined
William R. Cline

Equilibrium Exchange Rates for Global Economic Growth
Rudiger Dornbusch

Greening the GATT
Daniel C. Esty

Foreign Direct Investment in the United States, Third Edition
Edward M. Graham and Paul R. Krugman

Global Competition Policy
Edward M. Graham and J. David Richardson

International Monetary Policymaking in the United States, Germany, and Japan
C. Randall Henning

The New Europe in the World Economy
Gary Clyde Hufbauer

Western Hemisphere Economic Integration
Gary Clyde Hufbauer and Jeffrey J. Schott

The United States as a Debtor Country
Shafiqul Islam

China in the World Economy
Nicholas R. Lardy

Measuring the Costs of Protection in Japan
Yoko Sazanami, Shujiro Urata, and Hiroki Kawai

The Uruguay Round: An Assessment
Jeffrey J. Schott

The Future of the World Trading System
John Whalley

Trade and the Environment: Setting the Rules
John Whalley and Peter Uimonen

Equilibrium Exchange Rates: An Update
John Williamson

For orders outside the US and Canada please contact:

Longman Group UK Ltd.
PO Box 88
Harlow, Essex CM 19 5SR
UK

Telephone Orders: 0279 623925
Fax: 0279 453450
Telex: 817484